Also by Claudia Black
Published by Ballantine Books:

"IT WILL NEVER HAPPEN TO ME!"
"IT'S NEVER TOO LATE TO HAVE A HAPPY
  CHILDHOOD"
DOUBLE DUTY: Dual Dynamics Within the Chemically
  Dependent Home

DOUBLE DUTY

Sexually Abused

Dual Dynamics Within the
Chemically Dependent Home

Claudia Black

BALLANTINE BOOKS • NEW YORK

Copyright © 1990 by Claudja, Inc.

All rights reserved under International and Pan-American Copyright Conventions. Published in the United States of America by Ballantine Books, a division of Random House, Inc., New York, and simultaneously in Canada by Random House of Canada Limited, Toronto. This book consists of portions of *Double Duty: Dual Dynamics Within the Chemically Dependent Home* originally published by Ballantine Books, a division of Random House, Inc. in 1990.

Grateful acknowledgment is made to the following for permission to reprint previously published material:

ADULT CHILDREN OF ALCOHOLICS: "The Original Laundry List." Reprinted by permission of Tony A., co-author of *The ACOA Experience.*

ALCOHOLICS ANONYMOUS WORLD SERVICES, INC.: The Twelve Steps and Traditions of Alcoholics Anonymous are reprinted by permission of Alcoholics World Services, Inc. Permission to reprint and adapt The Twelve Steps and Traditions does not mean that AA has reviewed or approved the contents of this publication, nor that AA agrees with the views expressed herein. AA is a program of recovery from alcoholism. Use of The Twelve Steps and Traditions in connection with programs which are patterned after AA but which address other problems does not imply otherwise.

THE FREE PRESS: Figure entitled "Alcohol Addiction" from *Alcohol Problems and Alcoholism* by James E. Royce. Copyright © 1981 by The Free Press. Reprinted with permission of The Free Press, a division of Macmillan, Inc.

NATIONAL COUNCIL ON ALCOHOLISM AND DRUG DEPENDENCE, INC.: "Do You Have the Disease of Alcoholism?" reprinted by permission of the National Council on Alcoholism and Drug Dependence, Inc. Preprinted copies are available from NCAAD, 12 West 21st Street, New York, NY 10010.

ST. MARTIN'S PRESS, INC. AND SUSAN SCHULMAN LITERARY AGENCY, INC.: "Relationship Addiction" from *Women Who Love Too Much* by Robin Norwood. Copyright © 1985 by Robin Norwood. First published in hardcover by Jeremy P. Tarcher, Inc., Los Angeles. Reprinted by permission of St. Martin's Press, Inc. and Susan Schulman Literacy Agency, Inc.

SIMON & SCHUSTER, INC.: "Are You a Food Addict?" from *The Recovery Sourcebook* by Barbara Yoder. Copyright © by Wink Books. Reprinted by permission of Simon & Schuster, Inc.

Library of Congress Catalog Card Number: 90-34167

ISBN 0-345-37632-3

Manufactured in the United States of America

First Edition: October 1990
First Mass Market Edition: March 1992

In memory of my brother, Doug,
the inspiration for *Double Duty*

Contents

Preface

Dear Reader:

After each book I have written I am never certain where my professional work and personal growth will take me next. When *It Will Never Happen to Me* was published in 1981, it represented an exploration in uncharted territory—it contributed to the start of something new—the Adult Children of Alcoholics movement.

While there has been a proliferation of books about Young and Adult Children of Alcoholics since that time, it is important to recognize that the Adult Children of Alcoholics movement is still very young. We are only beginning to understand the complexity of the actual trauma within the dysfunctional family systems that so many Adult Children have experienced, and the various ways this has compromised their adulthood.

Over the years thousands of Adult Children have begun their process of self-healing. There have been many wonderful miracles. Yet, as I've watched people moving through their recovery, I've also seen many individuals hit a baffling, impenetrable wall that halted their progress. There seemed to be a missing link or another piece to the puzzle.

A very big piece of what I believe causes such blockage is the experience of double duty. It is through exploring these issues that we will be able to recognize and confront these challenging dynamics and move on to lasting recovery.

One of the key premises of the ACOA recovery process is putting the past behind us. That only occurs when the truth of one's experience is acknowledged. Up to this time in the evolution of the ACOA movement, the stories told—and as a result the issues addressed—have tended to be very generalized. This stage of emphasizing the experiences all ACOAs have in common has been incredibly valuable. However, now that many Adult Children have spent several years in recovery from their ACOA issues, I believe it is time to explore how Adult Children differ from each other. And that difference is what *Double Duty* is all about.

During the past decade I've taught workshops and conducted professional training sessions from Seattle to Kansas City and Boston to Rio de Janeiro, Tokyo, and Garmish, West Germany. One recurring theme has struck a deep chord in me—the problems people have encountered because of what I've come to call "Double Duty/Dual Identity" issues. These are the intensified life experiences of ACOAs who not only have had to contend with the trauma of family alcoholism, but who have also had to defend against an additional powerful dynamic that profoundly affected their lives. The additional struggle might be with incest or physical disability, being gay or lesbian or a person of color. I met Adult Children who'd been physically abused; ACOAs who'd been sexually abused; ACOAs who had eating disorders; ACOAs who were also chemically dependent; ACOAs who'd been raised as the only child in the family nightmare.

The questions such individuals posed in my workshops/trainings all coalesced in the same psychological pool: "How do I deal with the impact of being a survivor of sexual abuse as I address my ACOA issues?" And the question so many are asking: "Why am I having such a hard time in therapy?"

All of these individuals were experiencing the same things—when they looked in the mirror they saw their identities expressed in two or more ways. And in that recognition—in that process of looking in the mirror and unearthing their own histories—they began to recognize that what was reflected back to them was not one, but two equally powerful dynamics. These had created profoundly disruptive internal messages that they knew had to be recognized and healed before they could make peace with themselves.

I believe that no human being deserves the shame that is often created by these Double Duty/Dual Identity situations. No one deserves to live with the depth of fear, loneliness, deprivation, and isolation found in the lives of the people throughout this book. I believe that we all deserve to have choices in our lives. In *Double Duty* my intention has been to offer validation to the unique life experiences of these Adult Children and, equally important, to offer an explanation for that "wall" so many ACOAs run into during their recovery process.

It is my hope that the life stories in this book will help all Adult Children come to believe that, no matter how traumatic their past experiences, recovery is possible.

By openly exploring their Double Duty/Dual Identity issues, the contributors have displayed not only rare courage and generosity—they have also reached deeply into themselves and discovered yet another level of their own recovery.

It takes a great deal of inner strength to tell others these kinds of stories and to share so openly. The contributors said things they had never previously spoken, written, or shared in any manner. In opening their souls at such a deep level, they ran the gamut of emotions. They cried; they laughed; they became angry; they grew sad. But as they revealed their vulnerability, they also trusted in the process of their recovery.

At the beginning of our work together nearly all the contributors were strangers to me—though not in spirit. Most of them volunteered their stories for the book at workshops or conferences.

There has been a tendency by some to be critical of Adult Children for not moving forward more quickly in recovery. My hope is that *Double Duty* will offer validation to those who have not been able to move on because they first needed a clearer perspective from which to examine their lives. I hope that this book will promote both an expanded sense of self for Double Duty/Dual Identity survivors and a greater understanding of the genuine complexity of the Double Duty/Dual Identity issues by families, friends, and therapists.

I hope that *Double Duty* will be another step in the

process of recovery for all of us. I am honored by the trust that so many of you have placed in me.

I am with you in spirit.

Claudia Black
October 1990

Acknowledgments

I would like to express my gratitude and say thank you, first and foremost, to all the contributors who participated in this project. While only three life stories appear in this final book, I am also greatly indebted to many other contributors who offered stories that were not included. Each of your individual contributions helped me to better understand the particular Double Duty/Dual Identity issues presented here.

I would also like to thank my friends and colleagues who gave me such thoughtful feedback: Dr. Leslie Drozd and Victoria Danzig.

Barbara Shor, a heartfelt thanks for the final hand polishing of my prose.

Cheryl Woodruff, my editor who walked this journey with me.

DOUBLE DUTY

Sexually Abused

1

The Challenge of
Double Duty/Dual Identity

*Out of the seven of us kids, three are alcoholic, two are
married to alcoholics, and the other two are just all
screwed up.*

—*Adult Child*

Adult Children of Alcoholics (ACA or ACOA) is
a term that describes an adult person who was
raised in a family affected by parental chemical
dependency and co-dependence.

The wording is not meant to imply that this adult-age
person behaves as a child. It means that within this
person there is an inner spirit—an inner child—who
has been hurt and who now needs to be recognized,
validated, and healed. Inside this Adult Child is an
adult-age person who is as emotionally vulnerable as a
nine-year-old or a twelve-year-old. I picture the Adult
Child as a nine-year-old with thirty-five years of pain
or a twelve-year-old with forty-five years of pain.

The phrase *Adult Children* acknowledges that within
each of these adult-age individuals there is a child who

has difficulty experiencing a healthy life until he (or she) is able to speak the truth about his childhood and free himself from the bondage of his past. Until this recognition and healing of the past occurs, Adult Children are destined to continue reliving old scripts.

The ACOA movement has allowed thousands of people to recover from the pain of their childhoods. It has given them hope and a sense of direction. It has offered them choices about how they will continue to live their lives from now on.

I first used the term *Adult Children of Alcoholics* (*ACA or ACOA*) in 1977, in the initial phases of the development of the concept. Since then the phrase and its acronym have moved through a variety of changes.

Today, when people speak of ACOAs, they're usually referring to Adult Children who were raised in chemically dependent families. Until recently, "alcoholism" is the term that has been most widely used in the field of substance abuse to describe chemically dependent families. However, over the past decade, "chemical dependency" has become a much more commonly used phrase because it covers both alcohol and other drug dependencies. To be even more inclusive, some professionals use the phrase *Adult Children of Addicted Families*.

More and more people are identifying with Adult Children characteristics—whether or not they were raised in alcoholic families. And because so many are also finding answers in the process of recovery used by ACOAs, this concept has expanded even further until it has become "Adult Children of Dysfunctional Families."

How to Recognize the Adult Child

- We become isolated and afraid of other people, especially authority figures.
- We are frightened by anger and any personal criticism.
- We judge ourselves harshly and have low self-esteem.
- We don't act—we react.
- We are dependent personalities who are terrified of abandonment.
- We will do anything to hold on to a relationship. This is the way we avoid feeling the pain of our parents not having been there for us emotionally.
- We become alcoholics, marry them, or do both. Or we find another compulsive personality, such as a workaholic or an overeater, with whom we continue to play out our fear of abandonment.
- We have become addicted to excitement from years of living in the midst of a traumatic and often dangerous family soap opera.
- We live life from the viewpoint of victims or rescuers and are attracted to victims or rescuers in our love, friendship, and career relationships.
- We confuse love with pity and tend to love people whom we can pity and rescue.
- We felt responsible for the problems of our unstable families, and as a result we do not feel entitled to live independent lives now.
- We get guilt feelings if we stand up for ourselves instead of giving in to others.
- We became approval seekers and lost our own identities in the process.
- We have an overdeveloped sense of responsibility to-

ward others, but we rarely consider our responsibility
to ourselves.
• We had to deny our feelings in our traumatic childhoods. This estranged us from all our feelings, and
  we lost our ability to recognize and express them.

This collection of statements is often referred to as
the "Laundry List for Adult Children." It exists in
many forms and is widely used in Adult Child self-help
groups. See appendix 6, pages 172–174, for another
variation.

Troubled Families

If you identify with many of the issues presented in the
laundry list, it is likely that you were raised in a chemically dependent or otherwise dysfunctional family.
What is true for Adult Children from addicted families
is also true for people from other kinds of troubled
families. These family systems are usually affected by
denial, rigidity, isolation, and shame. Sometimes Adult
Children can identify the primary source of the dysfunction in the family, sometimes not. It isn't as important to know exactly what caused the dysfunction as
it is to recognize the messages internalized during your
childhood that you are still reenacting today.

The common denominator for those who identify with
Adult Child characteristics is a pervading sense of loss.
These are people who as children were raised in fami-
lies where they experienced loss on a chronic basis.
That loss may have been due to physical abandonment,
emotional abandonment, or both.

Children from alcoholic and other troubled families

could also be referred to as "Children of Denial" or "Children of Trauma." As young people they learned to continually deny, minimize, rationalize, and discount their feelings and their experiences. Some learned to lie blatantly to protect themselves or their family image. Others learned simply not to speak up—so the truth was never told.

Living with such chronic loss—at a time in their young lives when they were developing their identity and sense of self-worth—was very traumatic. Too often people forget that we are referring to children of three, seven, eleven, fifteen years of age. The trauma in their lives has been easy to discount because those around them discounted it and also because COAs demonstrate such phenomenal survivorship skills.

For decades the treatment focus of the chemically dependent family was the alcoholic; it was not until the problems of the emotionally dependent spouse or partner of the alcoholic were recognized that the term *co-alcoholic* was coined. Co-alcoholic implied that the partner was also significantly affected by the disease on psychological, mental, social, and even physical levels as a result of being in a close relationship with a chemically dependent person. Because of this, it was believed that these individuals also needed and deserved treatment and a recovery process of their own. The term "co-dependent" soon replaced "co-alcoholic" because alcoholics were increasingly being referred to as "chemically dependent."

Today, co-dependency no longer reflects only those traits exhibited by the spouse or partner of an alcoholic. It also refers to people whose behavior is characterized by the numbing of feelings, by denial, low self-worth, and compulsive behavior. It manifests itself in relationships when you give another person power over your self-esteem. The ACOA movement was the precursor of the co-dependency movement.

At a recent national conference on co-dependency, a group of 1,800 educators agreed upon a definition of the term. Co-dependency was seen as "a pattern of painful dependency on compulsive behaviors and on approval from others in an attempt to find safety, self-worth, and identity." However, although the great majority of Adult Children manifest co-dependency traits, not all co-dependents are ACOAs.

Double Duty is a book for anyone who identifies with being an Adult Child, no matter what the cause of trauma in the family.

The Healthy Family

Some people question whether or not any of us comes from a healthy family. Cartoonist Jennifer Berman brilliantly captures this sentiment in her cartoon that shows a nearly empty auditorium with a large sign in the back reading, "ADULT CHILDREN OF NORMAL PARENTS ANNUAL CONVENTION."

Although it is true that anyone reading the laundry list could identify with some of the statements on it, only those who have been raised with chronic loss are able to identify with most of them. Such individuals actively need to address what their past means—and how it continues to affect them—in order to create greater choice and balance in their present lives.

Still, it is my belief that there are indeed healthy family systems. In fact, it is often recovering Adult Children who are creating those healthy systems today.

All of us can benefit by looking at the behavioral patterns we encountered in our birth families so that we can take responsibility for reshaping our lives differently as adults. One of the greatest gifts of the Adult Children's movement is the energy directed toward understanding and creating the dynamics of a healthy family.

Since many Adult Children often lack an understanding of what is normal or healthy in family life, the following lists may be helpful.

IN A NURTURING FAMILY . . .

- People feel free to talk about inner feelings.
- All feelings are okay.
- The person is more important than performance.
- All subjects are open to discussion.
- Individual differences are accepted.
- Each person is responsible for his/her own actions.
- Respectful criticism is offered along with appropriate consequences for actions.
- There are few "shoulds."
- There are clear, flexible rules.
- The atmosphere is relaxed.
- There is joy.
- Family members face up to and work through stress.
- People have energy.
- People feel loving.
- Growth is celebrated.
- People have high self-worth.
- There is a strong parental coalition.

IN A DYSFUNCTIONAL FAMILY . . .

- People compulsively protect inner feelings.
- Only "certain" feelings are okay.
- Performance is more important than the person.
- There are many taboo subjects, lots of secrets.
- Everyone must conform to the strongest person's ideas and values.
- There is a great deal of control and criticism.
- There is punishment, shaming.
- There are lots of "shoulds."
- The rules are unclear, inconsistent, and rigid.
- The atmosphere is tense.
- There is much anger and fear.
- Stress is avoided and denied.
- People feel tired, hurt, and disappointed.
- Growth is discouraged.
- People have low self-worth.
- Coalitions form across generations.[1]

Alcoholism as a Disease

Some people in recovery have come to an understanding of the disease process of chemical dependency. Yet this concept is confusing to those who may recognize that their parent was dependent on alcohol or other drugs but still perceive that parent as being willful or bad. What parents do as a result of their chemical dependency may be bad, but it is because of the disease process that they have lost the opportunity for choice. I don't know what those parents would have been like had they not been chemically dependent. But I do know that they would have had a greater range of choices about how they handled their parenting and how they expressed those choices.

Alcoholism has been a part of human history since the beginning of recorded time. But to the astonishment of many, it has been barely twenty-five years since it was formally recognized as a disease. Many professionals think of 1956 as the date of recognition for the disease concept, for it was in that year that the American Medical Association (AMA) first endorsed the admission of alcoholics to general hospitals. It was a major step toward formal recognition of alcoholism as a disease, but that did not occur officially until November 26, 1966, when the house of delegates of the AMA, meeting in Houston, Texas, adopted the following resolution:

> Whereas, the American Medical Association of 1966 recognized that alcoholism is a disease that merits the serious concern of all members of health professions; and whereas, alcoholism is recognized as a serious major health problem throughout the land; therefore be it RESOLVED, that the American Medical Association identifies alcoholism as a complex disease and as such recognizes that the medical components are medicine's responsibility. Such recognition is not intended to relieve the alcoholic of moral or legal responsibility, as provided by law, for any acts committed when inebriated; nor does this recognition preclude civil arrest and imprisonment, as provided by the law, for antisocial acts committed when inebriated.

Alcohol Addiction: The Progression of the Disease

EARLY STAGE

OCCASIONAL RELIEF DRINKING

CONSTANT RELIEF DRINKING COMMENCES

INCREASE IN ALCOHOL TOLERANCE

SNEAKING DRINKS

ONSET OF MEMORY BLACKOUTS (IN SOME PERSONS)

URGENCY OF FIRST DRINKS

AVOID REFERENCE TO DRINKING

INCREASING DEPENDENCE ON ALCOHOL

CONCERN/COMPLAINTS BY FAMILY

FEELINGS OF GUILT

PREOCCUPATION WITH ALCOHOL

MEMORY BLACKOUTS INCREASE OR BEGIN

DECREASE OF ABILITY TO STOP DRINKING WHEN OTHERS DO

LOSS OF CONTROL

MIDDLE STAGE

GRANDIOSE AND AGGRESSIVE BEHAVIOR OR EXTRAVAGANCE

ALIBIS FOR DRINKING

FAMILY MORE WORRIED, ANGRY

PERSISTENT REMORSE

GOES ON WAGON

CHANGE OF PATTERN

EFFORTS TO CONTROL FAIL REPEATEDLY

TELEPHONITIS

TRIES GEOGRAPHICAL ESCAPE

HIDES BOTTLES

LOSS OF OTHER INTERESTS

PROMISES OR RESOLUTIONS FAIL

FURTHER INCREASE IN MEMORY BLACKOUTS

DENIAL

FAMILY AND FRIENDS AVOIDED

UNREASONABLE RESENTMENTS

WORK AND MONEY TROUBLES

NEGLECT OF FOOD

TREMORS AND EARLY MORNING DRINKS

LATE STAGE

PROTECTS SUPPLY

PHYSICAL DETORIORATION

DECREASE IN ALCOHOL TOLERANCE

IMPAIRED THINKING

ONSET OF LENGTHY INTOXICATIONS

DRINKING WITH INFERIORS

OBSESSION WITH DRINKING

INDEFINABLE FEARS

UNABLE TO INITIATE ACTION

VAGUE SPIRITUAL DESIRES

ALL ALIBIS EXHAUSTED

ETHICAL DETERIORATION

COMPLETE DEFEAT ADMITTED

OBSESSIVE DRINKING CONTINUES IN VICIOUS CIRCLES

Source: James Royce, *Alcohol Problems and Alcoholism* (New York: Macmillan/Free Press, 1981).

THE ROAD TO RECOVERY

ENLIGHTENED AND INTERESTING WAY
OF LIFE OPENS UP WITH ROAD
AHEAD TO HIGHER LEVELS THAN
EVER BEFORE

FULL APPRECIATION OF
SPIRITUAL VALUES

GROUP THERAPY AND MUTUAL HELP CONTINUE

CONTENTMENT IN SOBRIETY

FIRST STEPS TOWARD
ECONOMIC STABILITY

CONFIDENCE OF EMPLOYERS

INCREASE OF EMOTIONAL CONTROL

APPRECIATION OF REAL VALUES

FACTS FACED WITH COURAGE

REBIRTH OF IDEALS

NEW CIRCLE OF STABLE FRIENDS

NEW INTERESTS DEVELOP

ADJUSTMENTS TO FAMILY NEEDS

FAMILY AND FRIENDS APPRECIATE EFFORTS

REHABILITATION

DESIRE TO ESCAPE GOES

REALISTIC THINKING

RETURN OF SELF-ESTEEM

REGULAR NOURISHMENT TAKEN

DIMINISHING FEARS OF THE
UNKNOWN FUTURE

APPRECIATION OF POSSIBILITIES
OF NEW WAY OF LIFE

CARE OF PERSONAL APPEARANCE

START OF GROUP THERAPY

ONSET OF NEW HOPE

PHYSICAL OVERHAUL BY DOCTOR

GUILT REDUCTION

RIGHT THINKING BEGINS

SPIRITUAL NEEDS
EXAMINED

MEETS HAPPY SOBER ALCOHOLICS

STOPS TAKING
ALCOHOL

TOLD ADDICITON CAN BE ARRESTED

LEARNS ALCOHOLISM IS AN ILLNESS

HONEST DESIRE FOR HELP

Modified from M. M. Glatt

The *Random House Dictionary* defines disease as "a disordered or incorrectly functioning . . . system of the body resulting from the effect of genetic or developmental errors, . . . poisons, . . . [or] toxicity."

Clearly, alcohol and other drugs are poisons to the body. Although not everyone who drinks experiences delirious effects, 8 to 12 percent of our adult population becomes dependent psychologically and often physically.

Yet alcoholism is no more a single disease entity than cancer. Many people are confused about alcoholism because there is not one specific pattern of behavior typical to the alcoholic. Alcoholics often differ in their styles of drinking, and the consequences of their drinking vary widely. Some alcoholics drink daily; others drink in episodic patterns; some stay dry for long intervals between binges. Some drink enormous quantities of alcohol; others do not. Some alcoholics drink only beer; some drink only wine; others choose distilled liquor. Many consume a wide variety of alcoholic beverages and possibly other drugs as well. Today, many alcoholics are dual-addicted—that is, they are addicted to alcohol and another drug, such as marijuana, cocaine, or a prescription pill.

Although alcoholism appears very early in the lives of some people, for others it takes years to develop. Some claim to have started drinking alcoholically from their first drink. Many others report drinking for years before crossing over the "invisible line" that separates social drinking from alcoholic drinking.

While there are exceptions and variations to the rule, most alcoholics experience a progression in their disease. The preceding "dip chart," originally published in 1974 by British physician M.M. Glatt, describes the progression of both the active disease and recovery.

As you read the life stories in the chapters that follow, you will see children responding to parents who are in different stages of the disease. Typically, alcoholism is not even identifiable until someone is in at least middle-stage chemical dependency. This means that children live with the insidious effects of the disease long before it is recognized as a real problem. When alcohol or other drug usage does become more recognizable as a key contributor to the problem, denial, misinformation, and stigma have already spread throughout the family system. Family members have learned their adaptive roles and are trying to survive. At this point, many children still don't recognize their parents' chemical dependency in spite of its blatancy because they have learned the rules of all dysfunctional families: 1) Don't talk; 2) Don't feel; 3) Don't trust; 4) Don't think; 5) Don't ask questions. There is also another problem— very often many family members don't understand alcoholism well enough to recognize it when it smacks them in the face.

Not every alcoholic will experience all of the symptoms shown on the chart, nor do the symptoms have to occur in the exact order presented. In addition, the disease's rate of progression varies. Alcoholism tends to be more rapid for some individuals in some races, which is probably the result of a physiological predisposition. Generally, the progression of the disease is faster for women and young alcoholics than for men. Some alcoholics take thirty or forty years to reach the ''chronic'' late stage. Others remain in the middle stage indefinitely. However, my clinical experience has demonstrated that Children of Alcoholics who have problems with alcohol move through the progression much more quickly than those with alcohol problems which are not biologically related.

Children within the family may be affected differently. One reason for the variance is birth order. As each child is born, he or she enters the family life story at a different point in the progression of the disease. Should they enter the family prior to the onset of chemical dependency or in the earlier stages of the disease, they are more likely to have had attention focused on them as individual children rather than merely as objects, and they would have experienced greater stability and predictable adult behavior in their earlier years. This frequently creates a greater internal sense of security than that experienced by siblings who enter the family drama at a later point.

But we must recognize that children are not affected only by the chemically dependent parent. They are equally affected by the entire family system, which includes the nonchemically dependent parent (if there is one). Most typically, as the chemically dependent partner moves through the disease progression, the nonaddicted spouse will become more and more preoccupied with the partner's drinking and what that person is thinking and doing. The spouse often begins to display "enabling" behavior to the alcoholic by learning to deny what is going on. Also, the spouse keeps trying to control the alcoholic's behavior, often without understanding what is actually happening.

As the disease progresses, the co-dependent mate becomes angry and depressed and often seeks forms of escape to handle his or her own escalating confusion, guilt, and helplessness. It is no surprise that the children often get left behind in the shuffle and end up living without the focus and attention they need. Their lives are distorted by the unrealistic expectations, unpredictability, rigid (or total lack of) discipline, chaos, tense silence, and abuse from both the alcoholic and the co-dependent parent.

Effects of Family Roles

Children in chemically dependent families do whatever they can to withstand the losses they are experiencing in the family environment. Surprisingly, most children from troubled families have the ability to "look good" to outsiders despite what may be happening in the home. Unfortunately, for the most part looking good is based on survivorship and denial. Children accommodate themselves to whatever environment they are being raised in. They keep trying to bring consistency, structure, and safety into a household that is unpredictable, chaotic, and frightening. To do this they adopt certain roles, or a mixture of these roles, in the family. My research indicates that 60 percent of COAs identify themselves as the *overly responsible* (hero) child; 63 percent identify themselves as the family *placater*; 40 percent identify with being the *adjuster* (lost child); and 20 percent identify with being the *acting-out* child (scapegoat).[2] As the statistics indicate, most people identify with more than one role or recognize that at certain times their roles switch. Many people from other types of troubled families identify with those roles as well.

THE RESPONSIBLE CHILD

This is the child who takes responsibility for whatever is tangible in the environment—people, places, and things. This is the child who sets the table, puts dinner on the table, and sees to it that the children are all sitting down with the right expressions on their faces before the alcoholic parent gets to the table. This is the child known as the "little adult," or the "household top sergeant."

Responsible children become their own parent, a parent to their siblings, and a parent to the parents. It is extremely difficult for these children to be perceived as being in any emotional trouble because, externally, they look very good. They often become the face for the chemically dependent home. Their appearance says to themselves and to the community that everything is just fine here, things are under control.

CORE EMOTIONS:
Fear
Loneliness
Hurt
Powerlessness
Anger
Sadness
Embarrassment

STRENGTHS:
Organized
Goal-oriented
Self-disciplined
Leadership ability

Willingness to take charge
Decisive

DEFICITS:
Difficulty with listening
Difficulty with following
Difficulty with negotiating
Difficulty with asking for help, input, or advice
Difficulty playing
Perfectionist behavior

EMOTIONALLY:
Serious
Rigidly removed from feelings
Perceives experiencing feelings as a loss of control

THE ADJUSTER

This is the child who doesn't want to be emotionally or socially invested in what is occurring in the family. These children shrug their shoulders and say, "It doesn't bother me. I don't care."

Adjusters spend their time trying to be less visible and, as a result, don't draw much attention to themselves—negative or positive. An adjuster is often referred to as the "lost child." These children also don't have the ability to cry out for help or to say there is something wrong in their lives. They take the stance of, "I can handle it. I'm tough. I can adjust. If I am not invested, then I am not going to get hurt. Just don't think about it."

STRENGTHS:
Flexibility
Ability to adjust

Easygoing attitude and personality
Not willing to be preoccupied with negativity

DEFICITS:
Inability to lead
Inability to initiate
Fearful of making decisions
Inability to see options
Reacts without thinking

EMOTIONALLY:
Aloof
Withdrawn, or can be pleasant as a defense mechanism

THE PLACATER

This is the "household social worker," the child who takes responsibility for the emotional well-being of all the family members. This child takes on the task of reducing and minimizing the expressed and sometimes unexpressed fears, sadness, anger, and embarrassment of the whole family. Placaters are warm, caring, empathetic young people. Again, they are expert at not drawing attention to themselves as children in need.

STRENGTHS:
Warm
Caring
Empathetic
Good listener
Nice smile
Ability to give
Sensitive to others

DEFICITS:

Difficulty with receiving
Inability to focus on self
Incredible guilt for self-focus
Highly tolerant of inappropriate behavior
Highly fearful of mistakes

EMOTIONALLY:

Extremely warm and interested in others
Closed to their own feelings of inadequacy, fear, and
    sadness

THE ACTING-OUT CHILD

This is the one who is willing to scream to the world
that there is something wrong here. Unfortunately, even
when this child does so, the alcoholism may still not
get identified or addressed. This child challenges authority more blatantly than the others and, as a result,
is more likely to be in trouble in school and in the
community. In reality, acting-out children tend to suffer
less from denial than the others in the chemically dependent family. They are closer to knowing the truth
and are acting out the dysfunction of the family.

STRENGTHS:

Good leadership ability, recognizing they just lead in
    the wrong direction
Less denial, closer to the truth
Less apt to subscribe to the "Don't talk" rule
Creative

DEFICITS:

Hurtful expression of anger

Greater lack of social skills

Intrusive with others

Greater difficulty entering the mainstream of life due
   to tendency to challenge authority and unwillingness
   to follow directions

EMOTIONALLY:

Angry

Most fearful of their sadness and their fears

Acting-out children, more than the other role players,
are more likely to enter into an addictive process at a
younger age. If their addiction is chemical dependency,
they will progress through the stages of their drug/al-
cohol dependency at a younger age. Consequently they
may also die earlier from those dependencies—or get
well sooner.

Whether these role players are drawing positive or
negative attention to themselves, or being invisible, all
of these ACOAs are learning such rules as:

Don't talk honestly.

Don't express your feelings.

Your feelings don't count.

You are not important.

You can't trust anybody.

No one will be there for you.

Your perceptions aren't accurate.

There is no time to play.

Other people's needs are more important than your own.

These roles typify the experiences of children who
have lived with great loneliness, fear, sadness, disap-

pointment, anger, guilt, and shame. They are COAs who have lived and struggled with powerlessness. The roles they have adopted are the ways they learned to mask their chronic losses and their different methods of coping with their feelings.

The Adult Child and Progression

It is important to understand that what has been seeded in a dysfunctional childhood takes a grave toll in dramatic ways in adulthood. And it is in adulthood that these problems finally begin to surface. There are many symptoms:

- Depression
- Inability to develop or maintain a healthy relationship
- Remaining victimized within a destructive relationship
- Poor parenting skills
- Inability to actualize one's potential or talent, inability to experience accomplishments in spite of proven abilities
- Compulsive behaviors
- Addictions

The problems of Adult Children are rarely identified until the individuals are at least in their late twenties or early thirties. When seventeen-, eighteen-, and nineteen-year-old Adult Children begin to leave their families of origin, there is usually no time for quiet self-reflection. At this point many ACOAs hold on to their survivorship skills for dear life and, as many put it, "move on," not thinking, not feeling, not talking about their growing-up years. Yet they usually continue to stay emotionally enmeshed with their families.

It is not until ACOAs begin to experience more of a normal daily routine in their lives that these issues become increasingly visible to themselves and possibly others. As with alcoholism, Adult Child issues escalate over time. But these problems don't tend to hit like a dramatic bolt of lightning. Adult Children are often deep in the throes of a troubling situation before they recognize that there is a problem.

Not recognizing a problem until it reaches the crisis stage is one of the core issues of ACOAs. This is because they have spent years learning to dismiss relevant cues and signals in order to survive. Such a capacity for denial can create an endless loop in which ACOAs are forever reacting to problems.

Another Adult Child issue that interferes with the process of seeking help is that, as young people, they learned that it was not safe or okay to ask for help. They came to believe that no one would be there for them if they did.

When we add up these three dynamics—that problems enter and escalate in our lives slowly; that we don't recognize a problem until it has reached the crisis stage; and that we don't trust the process of asking for help—we can begin to understand why it may have taken us such a long time to be able to address these issues.

Another significant factor in recovery for Adult Children is that, until the ACOA movement began, information about these problems and their solutions wasn't available. Our understanding of these dynamics did not begin until the late 1970s, and recovery resources have only been widely available since the mid-1980s.

It is very common for ACOAs to berate themselves for being so "old" before they began to recognize that they were Adult Children and see how it has affected their lives. Please remember that it doesn't matter how old you are when you begin your recovery. What matters is that you are here now and ready to begin this work. Recovery is possible for anyone at any age. To date, my oldest Adult Child was eighty-six, and most recently I met a woman who had just begun her Adult Child recovery at an enthusiastic seventy-five.

Beyond Survivorship

Denial has been a powerful part of every ACOA's life. If you've allowed yourself even a few thoughts about your dysfunctional or troubled family, you might at first have seen only your strengths. Adult Children are incredible survivors! As a youngster some of the strengths you learned were:

To take charge, to lead
To make adult decisions
To be self-reliant
To be autonomous
To solve problems creatively
To be a hard worker
To be loyal
To develop empathic skills
To develop your talents in art, writing, music, and so on, to provide a safe escape
To respond effectively in a crisis.

The list could go on and on.

We certainly deserve to feel good about our strengths however they were developed. Yet by ignoring what it was we didn't learn, our lives remain very limited. It is by acknowledging what didn't get learned in our childhood, as well as discovering what we learned that is no longer useful, that Adult Children can establish a direction for recovery.

Adult Children need to explore their past, and in doing so, they need to identify the helpful and the hurtful aspects of their growing-up years. The skills that were helpful in the past, and that remain helpful today, can certainly support you in your recovery. However, that which is hurtful must be stopped and new behavior learned in its place.

For example, learning self-reliance may have been most helpful as a child. However, as an adult you may be self-reliant to the point where you totally exclude others, which leaves you feeling lonely and isolated. Moving out of the perception that only extremes are valid will allow you to maintain a healthy self-reliance while simultaneously learning how to become interdependent with others. Recovery means that you will now have the opportunity to make conscious decisions in your life.

People in recovery are highly critical of what they refer to as their co-dependent behavior when they were children and adolescents. We must remember that these were survival skills. I don't think it was possible for us to behave any differently under the circumstances at that time in our lives. Don't be critical of your survivor self. Be accepting of your courage and vulnerability under difficult circumstances. The key to healthy living in adulthood is to recognize when we are maintaining survival skills that no longer work for us. We need to let go of old behavior that interferes with enjoying the type of life we would like to live now. Remember, childhood survivor skills carried into adulthood can continue to maintain a co-dependent life-style.

Many Adult Children are hesitant about beginning their recovery because they don't want to blame their parents for what they see as their own adult problems. *Recovery is not a blaming process.* Rather, it is a process of examining and speaking your truths. It is the process of breaking your denial, of acknowledging and taking ownership of your feelings and your life. In doing so, you may need to acknowledge pain from childhood and to be specific about where that pain came from. However, the goal is not to blame, but to be able to break the rules that have kept you in denial and disengaged from your self. Adult Children are fiercely loyal and are often frightened of betraying their families. But if there is any betrayal here, it is of the chemical addiction and co-dependency. You aren't betraying those parts of your mother and father that loved you. I believe our parents truly want us to be healthy and happy, but often their afflictions have gotten in the way. The only true act of betrayal is when we betray ourselves by not speaking our own truth.

Resources for Recovery

Some people began working on their ACOA issues before the concept of Adult Children came into being. Special focus groups for the Adult Child did not begin to develop until the late 1970s. Until that time, when

people did seek help, many could not identify themselves as ''Adult Children.'' Although some individuals
were able to resolve issues related to their childhood
without this label, most people ignored the primary issues.

In 1976 and 1977, when I began my work with Adult
Children in southern California, Stephanie Brown was
also addressing the issues at the Stanford Alcohol
Clinic; and Sharon Wegscheider-Cruse, then in Minneapolis, was spreading the word about family alcoholism. In the late seventies in New York City a small
group of Twelve Step Al-Anon members met at the
Smithers Institute to form a new group called Hope for
Adult Children of Alcoholics. This first formal meeting
was also held under the auspices of Al-Anon.

At that time one of the members of this group, Tony
A., developed the original ''laundry list'' of Adult Child
symptoms (see appendix, pages 172-174, 187). This list
has become a mainstay for ACOA self-help groups
throughout the country. Over the next few years there
was some confusion about nonapproved literature at
meetings and whether or not Adult Children needed to
organize separate Al-Anon meetings for themselves. As
a result of such concerns, there are a few hundred Al-
Anon-affiliated Adult Child groups nationwide, while
several hundred other Twelve Step groups for Adult
Children exist that are not affiliated with Al-Anon.

TWELVE STEP GROUPS
You will see that many of the people in this book have
sought recovery through the use of various Twelve Step
programs, such as ACA Al-Anon, ACA/ACOA, non-
Al-Anon ACA/ACOA, traditional Al-Anon, Overeaters

Anonymous (OA), Cocaine Anonymous (CA), Narcotics Anonymous (NA), and others. These groups were spawned as an outgrowth of the oldest, largest ongoing self-help Twelve Step program in the world—Alcoholics Anonymous (AA). The groups that have followed in the path of AA, which began in 1935, have developed a spiritual self-help program based on AA's Twelve Steps and Twelve Traditions.

The self-help groups familiar to most Adult Children of Alcoholics are AA, ACA/ACOA Anonymous, ACA Al-Anon, Al-Anon, and Co-Dependents Anonymous (CODA). These particular groups are organized around Twelve Step meetings. They usually last an hour to an hour and a half (depending on the region of the country). They adhere to the leaderless group model and follow a similar format, with a different person directing the meetings each time. The group usually begins with a reading of the laundry list and the Twelve Steps, and this is followed by a qualifying discussion or a discussion of a selected topic chosen from the program literature.

In these meetings people speak from their own experiences. They talk about whatever is on their minds as it relates to addiction and recovery or to unhealthy behavior they have identified in themselves and are beginning to change. There is no cross talk—which means that no one is allowed to give advice or direct another person's process. No one is required to share. There are no dues or fees.

Twelve Step and other self-help groups offer people an opportunity to realize that their experiences and feelings are not unique, but that in fact their problems are very similar to those each group member has experienced at some time.

Another unifying aspect of recovery support groups is that they practice the rule of anonymity. Who you are by name is not what is important, and as a rule, last names are not used. As well, the information shared in the meeting is not to be disclosed outside the room. In this way no matter what your financial or social status, you are considered equal to all human beings who suffer from the same issues as yourself. Each participant is helped through the support and understanding of the group.

ACOA groups offer a simple program with guidelines for understanding your situation and suggested steps to help you develop and sustain the new strengths and capabilities needed to counteract the old internalized messages of your dysfunctional past. These groups also provide opportunities for social interaction and feedback from recovering peers.

Some Adult Children have also found resources through self-help groups that are not Twelve Step oriented. Often such alternatives may simply be a group of Adult Children who choose to get together and develop their own support network.

THERAPY AS A RESOURCE

My theory is that ACOAs who are addressing Double Duty/Dual Identity issues—where difficulty in trusting others is often primary—are most likely to feel safer in the one-to-one therapy process before they feel ready for a group. Many Double Duty/Dual Identity people may need individual therapy before they can effectively use group therapy, or they may find that using both simultaneously proves to be the most beneficial.

Many Adult Children like and benefit from the group model but prefer it to be led by a counselor, educator, or therapist. Educators and clinicians have readily responded to information and a model of treatment that is proving to be particularly helpful to Adult Children. Adult Children often begin their work with an educational, time-limited support group with a small number of other Adult Children led by a therapist. Such groups are usually highly structured in terms of their content and will be limited to a certain number of meetings. People often move into long-term group therapy after participating in such educational groups or individual therapy.

Each of us is an individual, and each of us is in a different place in our recovery. While some Adult Children choose to work on their issues in a more isolated fashion through reading, others are using support groups offered by their churches. Most people use a combination of resources, including different self-help groups, reading, pastoral and psychological counseling, and individual and group therapy. Above all, what is important is to choose a path of recovery that is right for you, that is safe, and that offers you exactly what you want.

It is also my hope that the counselors and therapists reading this book will recognize that, because different ACOAs experience the same issues with differing intensities, it is important to develop a greater respect for individual pacing in the therapeutic process. We may not necessarily be able to use the same treatment plan for each Adult Child. We need to start where the client is.

The Growth of the ACOA Movement

ACOA is a very young movement—one that developed from the grass-roots level. However, it commanded a great deal of media attention. In a very short period of time—approximately ten years—thousands of Adult Children self-help groups have been created, and hundreds of books are now available on the subject. Many therapists are now targeting their practices to serve this special client population. Elementary schools and high schools are developing support groups for young COAs. National advocacy groups such as the National Association for Children of Alcoholics are developing and offering resources. The concept of co-dependency, although not limited to ACOAs, has also emerged as an accepted phenomenon, and it too has created its own proliferation of books, organizations, and attention.

Conferences for ACOAs are now being routinely held in every city in the nation, and these command large audiences. Entertainers and famous athletes are speaking out about their personal experiences as ACOAs. Publishers in other countries are rapidly translating books on these topics so that recovery support will soon be available worldwide—from Japan to India, and from Germany to Uruguay.

Of course, as with any movement that seizes the imagination of so many, the ACOA movement has generated enough energy to create a strong counterreaction. There are individuals who genuinely believe that it is only a fad. There are individuals who say the ACOA movement is self-serving for a small group of professionals, or that it is the "yuppie disease," meaning that it isn't relevant to a mainstream population and therefore has no value. Some say it is composed of adults who want to blame others and not take responsibility for their own lives. The objections go on and on.

The loudest critics appear to be those who are often the most uninformed or misinformed. These individuals revel in taking a single word of knowledge and transforming it into a volume of misinformation. They are often very frightened and quite possibly in denial themselves. Often they are individuals who have not been willing to open up to their own vulnerabilities.

Yet, as in any movement, there are aspects that can be hurtful. There may be people who take advantage of the movement or who take advantage of Adult Children by attempting to simplify serious issues that need to be addressed in great depth. But throwing the baby out with the bathwater serves no purpose. Valid criticism does not invalidate the importance and the value of this movement.

There are people who have spent years in therapy who are still unable to address their core issues because their family-of-origin issues were discounted or ignored. There are thousands of people within our communities who are the "walking wounded" because their ACOA issues have not been recognized or addressed. Their pain, which has both a legitimate basis and the potential for resolution, was not allowed to emerge. These people were encouraged to discount their feelings and keep them hidden.

That denial does not have to continue. Today there are hundreds of thousands of people from all walks of life—from prisons and psychiatric facilities to schoolrooms and corporate boardrooms—who are benefiting from what we have learned about Adult Children and the process of recovery. Today, Adult Children can heal, learn to make choices, and accept responsibility for how they live their lives.

The ACOA movement developed because so many Adult Children have begun to recognize what they have in common with each other. For the first time in their lives they no longer feel alone and isolated. They no longer feel as if there is something inherently wrong with who they are. They understand that there are reasons for how they have lived their lives. Guilt, shame, loneliness, and fear have been lessened. Hope and joy have become a genuine part of lives once dominated by pain.

Adult Children are learning basic skills, such as identifying and expressing feelings, problem-solving, establishing boundaries, setting limits. They are learning to trust and find healthy ways to include others in their lives. As a result of this collective effort, resources such as self-help groups specifically oriented toward Adult Children and private therapy groups for Adult Children are now available nationwide.

Double Duty/Dual Identity

I have observed many Adult Children belittling and criticizing themselves for not moving through recovery as easily or as speedily as others they know. I have found that when ACOAs are unable to work through the process with as much ease or speed as they would like, it is often because of their need to identify and address multiple issues in recovery. People who have multiple issues often have an additional need to protect themselves, and this may be why they do not connect with self-help groups or the group therapy process as quickly as others.

This book describes in detail the process the child experiences in an alcoholic family. It also examines the special problems of multiple issues—which I call "Double Duty/Dual Identity" (DD/DI)—that these Adult Children face, and the step-by-step process of their recovery. We can no longer continue to apply generic recovery programs to all ACOAs. While general recovery information is most often what one needs to focus on in early recovery, in time an individual's unique life situation has to be and deserves to be addressed. By refusing to look at the specifics of an individual's experiences we can inadvertently trivialize the purpose of the entire movement.

The concept of Double Duty is not meant to encourage people to use their differentness to keep others away or to resist new opportunities. I believe we must first see our commonalities, and humble and comfort ourselves in the realization that we are not unique. Although we suffered separately, we have not suffered alone. Only after we have acknowledged this common ground should we take the time to explore what may have been unique to our experiences.

There are many reasons for differences among Adult Children. Birth order affects children differently, sex role expectations affect children differently. Who the chemically dependent parent is, and the dynamics of how co-dependency shows itself, create differences among ACOAs. While many areas merit exploration, in my research I have chosen to focus on nine specific Double Duty issues that offer a conceptual framework on which others may build.

Double Duty exists when a child has one major trauma-inducing dynamic in the family and there exists an additional dynamic that reinforces the consequences through added trauma or complexity. Sometimes the additional dynamic may be physical abuse; other times it might be a life circumstance such as being an only child. (Being an only child in and of itself doesn't have to lead to trauma; in fact, it can have many advantages. But in the context of an alcoholic or troubled family, being an only child is a major disadvantage.)

I envision the Double Duty COA as a small child, hunched over, dragging unwieldy boxes and overflowing bags of trauma, when suddenly a dump truck comes roaring up and adds another load of pain.

For instance, if there is a terminally ill sibling in a child's family, growing up can be quite traumatic. But it does not have to create lifelong trauma if there is a healthy family system to help the surviving child respond to the situation. However, put the same set of circumstances in an alcoholic or otherwise troubled family, and the child involved will suffer many long-lasting effects from both issues. This is what I mean by a Double Duty situation.

In order to endure such trauma and added complexity—simply in order to survive—this child has to toughen up much more than other children. In adulthood, such survivors are likely to have their defenses rigidly in place and their emotions very hardened.

By contrast, Dual Identity is a special form of Double Duty in which one has at least two equally commanding aspects to one's identity—such as being a COA and a person of color, or being a COA and gay or lesbian. It is like looking into a two-sided mirror and seeing one image of yourself on one side and an equally real but different image on the other side. Although the images are different, they are invisibly enmeshed. This leaves Adult Children even more confused about who they are and what is most important in their lives.

For an Adult Child to experience a full recovery it is important to recognize that, as an ACOA, there may be other, equally significant aspects of your identity that need to be recognized and addressed—beyond those of having been raised in a chemically dependent family.

Double Duty/Dual Identity are examples of the synergistic effect of multiple-core issues that many Adult Children experience. The added dynamics of Double Duty/Dual Identity often force children to protect themselves even further. As a result, issues such as not trusting, not feeling, fear of losing control, and an overwhelming sense of shame are experienced even more deeply. It then becomes much more difficult for the afflicted ACOA to ask for help or to feel any hope. Very often the feeling of being overwhelmed by emotion or of having frozen emotions greatly impedes the ability to connect with a recovery process.

There are many people who know they are Adult Children, who know resources are available, who may even truly want to change their lives—yet always find that something seems to get in the way when they try to connect with a helping resource or try to stay involved once they've found that resource. There are others who are so powerfully defended against their pain that their level of denial is too strong for them even to recognize that their lives could be better. Still others become stuck in the process of recovery and "spin their wheels." These are often the DD/DI people.

While there are many life experiences that might merit the Double Duty or Dual Identity label, I have chosen to examine sexual abuse in this particular book. I have by no means meant to discount other Double Duty/Dual Identity situations. In fact, it is my hope that the life stories included in this volume will offer validation not only to those who recognize aspects of themselves in the lives presented here, but to those who experience Double Duty/Dual Identity situations that we have not addressed.

CHILDREN WHO SUFFER FROM PHYSICAL AND SEXUAL ABUSE

Having one's physical being attacked, whether through hitting or slapping, or verbal or sexual abuse, is terribly traumatizing and creates many long-term problems. When chemical dependency is added to that family system, the trauma is exacerbated. The effects multiply rapidly and constitute a Double Duty phenomenon.

Although there are many similarities between physical abuse and childhood sexual abuse, I believe that each warrants its own chapter because there are also important differences. In both situations a child is being treated as an object rather than as a person. When the offender is using force, whether the weapon is a hand, a belt, or a sexual organ, the act is one of domination. Both forms of violence are perpetrated by those who are supposed to be caretakers of children, yet both behaviors clearly show disregard and disrespect for the child. In both physical and sexual abuse, the children are powerless and shamed.

Incest is more covert than physical abuse. It often remains hidden from other family members, conducted behind closed doors. Physical abuse is much more likely to be witnessed by others. There is a further difficulty in that society has always sanctioned physical punishment for children, and this complicates the issue of parental rights versus children's rights.

On the one hand, children who are abused are much more likely to believe that they have done something wrong and that they are rightfully being punished. They develop the belief that they deserve what they get in life. The child who is physically abused is responding to a blatantly hostile, angry person.

On the other hand, there has always been a social taboo against incest—although it has occurred for centuries. The message is that any type of sexual behavior with a child is illegal and immoral. To make matters worse, incest is often perpetrated by a family member under the guise of a loving relative who nevertheless insists on compliance with his or her demands.

Sexual abuse is the one topic in this book that has been written about extensively. Many fine books have been published on the dynamics of sexual abuse and healing for adult survivors. However, this chapter is also a reminder that often one is not only an incest survivor, but also an Adult Child of a chemically dependent family. For the recovery process to be effective, these dynamics must be recognized and addressed in their duality.

The contributors in *Double Duty: Sexual Abused* have demonstrated a lot of courage and strength in their lives. By speaking of their lives and recovery, others raised in families where sexual abuse occured may have an opportunity to deal with their silence, too. It is my hope that this book will offer greater validation and under-standing of the lives of sexual abuse survivors.

Notes

1. Found through ACOA Self-Help Literature. Original source unknown.
2. C. Black, S. Bucky, and S. Padilla, "The Interpersonal and Emotional Consequences of Being an Adult Child of an Alcoholic," *Journal of International Addictions* 21 (May 1986); 213–32.

Life
Stories

How to Use This Book

In *Double Duty: Sexually Abused*, I have illustrated
the issues of a particular Double Duty group through
the truth of their life stories. The participants are in
many different phases of recovery and have used different resources in the recovery process.

For the purposes of anonymity, all names have been
changed. Portions of stories have been altered to provide even further anonymity. Any resemblance to your
life, or to the life of someone you know, is coincidental
and most likely due to the myriad commonalities in
alcoholic and troubled families.

In many of these stories you might find yourself wish-
ing for additional information or wondering what happened next. Please recognize that the gaps that appear
in the stories may reflect gaps in the memories of the
contributors themselves. Some contributors chose not
to share aspects of their lives to protect anonymity and
to maintain personal boundaries. Moreover, the purpose of this book is to explore Double Duty/Dual Identity issues. In order to maintain this focus, it was not

possible to offer a more extensive description of each contributor's life.

It is very easy to identify with many of the Double Duty/Dual Identity variables in this book. My advice is to try not to become overwhelmed or preoccupied with the number of additional dynamics that have operated in your life. It is much more important to focus on acknowledging that there are legitimate reasons why you experience your life as you do. Coming from a Double Duty or Dual Identity background is one of those reasons. Always remember: You are not crazy. You are not at fault. Owning this will move you through recovery with a greater acceptance of yourself—one that will ultimately support a deeper level of healing.

Obviously *Double Duty: Sexually Abused* is a very serious book, and I pray that it is an equally sensitive book. As you read, think ahead to how you can best take care of yourself if you find you are feeling vulnerable, angry, or sad.

Who knows you are reading this book? Do you have someone trustworthy to talk with if the going gets rough? I believe it is very important to share your feelings with another Adult Child or a counselor or therapist at this time. You will undoubtedly be experiencing feelings and memories of experiences that you never realized had significance from your past, and the intensity of these emotions must not be denied.

Keeping a Journal. As you become immersed in the life stories of the contributors, you may find that keeping a journal can be extremely helpful in your own recovery work. You may want to underline or highlight the statements or themes in *Double Duty* that you find especially meaningful and relevant to your own life. Then use your journal to record your own personal history, memories, flashes of insight, and questions for further thought that emerge as a result of reading that particular passage in the book.

You may want to begin the journal work each time by first writing down the date. This will help you keep track of your own inner journey by following the trail of insights as they occur one by one. Next, you might transcribe the passage in the book (noting the page number) that is triggering your response.

Then, just let your process flow as it will. Simply write down whatever thought first pops into your head, and the next thought, and the next. Try not to be critical of what you're writing or how you're writing it—that makes no difference. What is important is what you are saying to yourself.

Just let the flow continue until you have nothing more to say at that point. Then, either continue reading the book or, if you find yourself fatigued, just stop for the day. Return to the reading and journaling process whenever it feels right to you. If you find passages in the book too painful to read, try not to be frightened by your feelings. Simply remind yourself that it is critical that you be truly aware of how personal the story you are reading has become for you.

You might want to wait a few days to read what you've written in your journal. You may find yourself surprised by what you've written and the depth of your own wisdom. New insights may be triggered by rereading your journal from time to time as you're working through *Double Duty.* You might also find it helpful to share some of your journal entries with your therapist. But keeping a journal is like having a private rendezvous with yourself—you may not wish to share it with anyone, and you don't have to.

Final Considerations. Double Duty was never meant to be read quickly—certainly not in one sitting. Read it slowly. And read it with the support of people who love you and who understand the nature of the issues you may be struggling with.

2

Sexual Abuse

*I learned to cry quietly, if at all. I would blank out or
drift off as if I weren't there. I felt dead.*

—Adult Child

The Prevalence of Incest

Incest is one of our most ancient social taboos. Today it is both illegal and considered abhorrent. Yet
it is commonly practiced in this country. According
to a *Los Angeles Times* survey, it is estimated that nearly
38 million adults were sexually abused as children.
Twenty-two percent of those questioned—27 percent of
the women and 16 percent of the men—said they had
been sexually abused as children.[1]

A survey of 250,000 cases, referred to a Child Sexual
Assault Treatment Program, indicates that one in every
three women and one in every seven men have been
sexually abused by the time they reach the age of eighteen.[2]

In one of the largest and most complex studies of this
type, Diana Russell, a Harvard sociologist, interviewed

more than nine hundred randomly chosen women about their childhood sexual experiences. She found that nearly four women in every ten had been sexually abused before the age of eighteen by an adult relative or acquaintance.[3]

While incest is a taboo, it is much more prevalent than people are willing to accept. The greater taboo seems to be talking about it. But because incest is so traumatizing, when it is shrouded in silence the trauma is exacerbated.

Although I am focusing on incest in this chapter, I have no intention of minimizing the results of other types of sexual abuse. The effect of any sort of sexual abuse is always serious. But keeping with the focus of this book, I will specifically address incest within chemically dependent families.

Chemical dependency and incest often coexist in the same family. Several small studies have documented that more than 50 percent of known incest victims have lived in homes where alcohol abuse was a major problem. In my own research, I've found that daughters of alcoholics were two times more likely to be incest victims than daughters from nonaddicted families, and 27 percent of the female Adult Children I surveyed reported incidents of incest.[4]

In a more recent study, Dan Sexton and Dr. Jon Conte of the University of Chicago found that among six hundred adult survivors of child sexual abuse, 60 percent were self-described Children of Alcoholics.[5]

This is not meant to imply that one causes the other. What it does suggest is that both frequently occur within the same family, and therefore the possibility that both issues may exist must be addressed and responded to.

This is important, because the treatment of recovery from one issue does not automatically offer a full recovery for the other.

How Incest Is Manifested

Incest is one form of childhood sexual abuse. Incest occurs when a person related to a child or in a parental role—a parent, aunt, uncle, grandparent, sibling, cousin, also a stepparent or one who assumes parenting duties—acts with sexual overtones and/or imposes sexual acts on a child to meet his or her own sexual/emotional needs and/or to superimpose his or her authority. It is an act of violence and selfishness, and it is a violation of a position of trust, power, and protection. Perpetrators seldom commit childhood sexual abuse solely to satisfy their own sexual needs. They do it to exercise power over someone. Incest is an abhorrent crime perpetrated on defenseless children. And it thrives on silence.

Because incest survivors have lived in silence so long, it may be helpful to describe some of the behavior that is to be considered sexually abusive. The following is an abbreviated list from Suzanne Sgroi, *Handbook of Clinical Intervention in Child Sexual Abuse:*

- Genital exposure by the adult to the child.
- Observation of child (watching a child undress, bathe, or urinate).
- Kissing. The adult kisses the child in a lingering or intimate way.
- Fondling. The adult fondles the child's breast, abdomen, genital area, inner thighs, or buttocks. The

child may similarly fondle the adult at his or her request.

- Masturbation. The adult masturbates while the child observes; the adult observes the child masturbating; mutual masturbation.
- Cunnilingus/fellatio—oral-genital contact.
- Finger or object penetration.
- Penis penetration. Penetration may be either of the anus rectal or the vaginal area—or both.[6]

Abusers use power, age, experience, and position to persuade, coax, bribe, and threaten their victims into doing things they are not old enough or emotionally mature enough to cope with or defend against. The perpetrator takes advantage of the child's emotional, social, or physical dependence on him/her. If the person who becomes sexual with the child is even just a few years older than the child, or holds a position of power or authority, it is considered to be sexual molestation; if the person is related to the child, it is incest. Both constitute sexual abuse.

Even if the victim doesn't try to stop it, *the child is not responsible for the sexual abuse.* Remember, a child who is the victim of incest usually has no place to escape to and is too frightened to tell. Children are too young and immature to make the kinds of decisions that are involved in this type of sexual behavior. It is the responsibility—and the fault—of the older, more powerful person.

It is common for victims to become confused about the abuse when they were not physically forced to comply. But incest is an insidious type of violence that often does not require physical force. However, that does not mean the children wanted it to happen.

Perpetrators often play on trust to coerce their victim into meeting their demands. It is well known that abusers often choose children starving for attention, warmth, and affection. Children from troubled families are prime victims because they are particularly desperate for any sign of attention and affection.

Even more stressful, the victims are often afraid the family will break up if they don't go along with what the perpetrator wants. The alcoholic family is already on such shaky ground that children are terrified of losing the little they still have. They feel that if the family were to break up, they would be responsible for it.

In addition, victims often fear they will not be believed if they tell. And that could well be true, for this is already a family where telling the truth is not supported. As if this weren't enough, the perpetrator often threatens to hurt the victim, another family member, or a pet if the child tells. For the child in an alcoholic home, this is just one more threatening consequence of asking for help or telling the truth.

Another form of incest is one that is less easy to identify—especially for Adult Children. This is covert, or emotional, incest. Although emotional incest may be less overt, it is extremely traumatizing. Children are seriously damaged by emotional incest such as

- When their parents talk about specific sexual acts.
- When there is chronic nudity or nudity at inappropriate times.
- When children are forced to hear or even watch adults having sex.

- When there is sexual name calling.
- When they live in constant fear of sexual abuse occurring in their lives.

Children from alcoholic families are even less able to defend themselves against their offenders. They have greater difficulty knowing what their feelings are. They have a greater fear in trusting their own perceptions and trusting others. They are more confused about what constitutes appropriate limits and boundaries. And their sense of shame is already much greater than that experienced by children from nonalcoholic families. These problems occur without sexual abuse. But when sexual abuse also becomes a part of their life experience, the effects are even more intense.

COAs have already had to deal with a wall of denial when they attempt to discern the truth about what is going on in their lives. They have had to deal with a sense of powerlessness over the alcoholism. And now this is all compounded by a sense of total powerlessness over their own bodies. They have learned that there is no safe place for them. They are locked in because there is no way for them to confront their offenders. Confrontation means shame, guilt, denial, abandonment, and the possibility of physical violence. They see no way to break out of the cycle of abuse.

Incest is an overwhelming, damaging, and humiliating assault on a child's mind, soul, and body. It is a major act of betrayal, for not only is the body violated, but the child's trust and love are violated as well. When sexual abuse takes place in an already dysfunctional alcoholic family, the likelihood of the abuse continuing is greater, which compounds the damage.

Abuse affects self-esteem, one's relationships with others, one's developing sexuality, the ability to trust others, and the ability to be successful. It also seriously endangers one's physical health. Children who have been sexually abused often learn to medicate their pain through the use of alcohol, other drugs, or food. It is not uncommon to see a person raised in an alcoholic family, and who has been sexually abused, become an overeater, bulimic, anorexic, or chemically dependent. Because abuse victims come to feel ashamed, guilty, powerless, depressed, afraid, and angry, they are often attracted to love partners who abuse them physically, verbally, and sexually.

Obviously this kind of emotional damage extracts a heavy toll. As the child matures, anger intensifies, depression deepens, thoughts about suicide become attempts, panic attacks and phobias become a part of life. Time alone does not heal these wounds. But as the following life stories demonstrate, recovery, and a different way of life, is possible no matter what has occurred in one's childhood.

Life Stories: Growing-Up Years

The following three stories concern Adult Children who were sexually abused as they were growing up.

Amy was sexually abused by her grandfather for seven years. But she was also the witness to drunken sexual displays by her parents all of her growing-up years. Cindy was sexually abused by her father, brother, and male acquaintances. Josh was sexually abused by his mother, physically abused by his father, and the witness of drunken nudity and drunken sexual displays between his parents.

The fact that Josh, Cindy, and Amy all became alcoholic does not mean that all incest victims become chemically dependent. Many do; but others do not. Remember, these are stories of ACOAs, people genetically and psychologically more likely to become alcoholic. When sexual violence is added to their lives, alcohol and other drugs become even more necessary to medicate the pain and fear.

AMY
Age: 48
Mother: Alcoholic
Father: Alcoholic
Abusers: Both parents, grandfather
Birth Order: Oldest of two
Raised: Rocky Mountain states
Socioeconomic Status: Working class

Amy's father had been drinking heavily ever since she could remember. Her mother's drinking didn't become as obvious until Amy was around eight or nine years old.

Amy grew up with extremely inappropriate sexual behavior modeled for her by her parents.

AMY: *"Can you imagine what it was like to have both your parents drunk, nude, and making love—with the lights on—on the living room couch, while you, an eight-year-old, and your four-year-old brother watch from the open stairway door, feeling guilty for watching, but watching with a kind of horrified fascination, unable not to watch?''*

This behavior on her parents' part was very common throughout Amy's childhood. Amy's reaction to this would be one of shame and anger, although she was unable to identify these feelings.

"One time after unwillingly watching my parents have sex, I grabbed a butcher knife and went out to the chicken house. I sat there crying and talking to the chickens. My father must have noticed I was gone, because he came out looking for me. When he found me, he asked me what I was doing with the knife. I told him I didn't know, so he took the knife away from me and told me to go to bed. I told him I didn't like hearing what he and Mom were doing.

"The next morning, he gathered the family together and told my brother and me that he and Mom had a right to do whatever they wanted. He was really, really angry. He said that we weren't to mention it again. And I never did.''

The "Don't talk" rule became a law. Amy's feeling self was turning to stone.

Amy's sexual confusion was compounded even more because she was a victim of incest at the hands of her paternal grandfather. From the time she was four and a half until she was eleven, her grandfather molested her on a regular basis.

"When I was young, my grandparents lived near us. My grandfather would frequently come to the house and ask permission to take me fishing. That was where the molestation would take place, out on the lake in the boat. My grandfather would fondle me, and I was expected to touch him also. This went on steadily for three years.

"The only way I could cope with what I know I must have been feeling at the time was to separate myself, to distance myself, from what was happening. I did what I could not to think and feel about it. I put my attention everywhere else I could.

"We finally moved away from that part of the country, and we saw my grandparents less frequently, but he still continued to molest me whenever they came to visit."

Amy's confusion and fear about what happened was made worse by the fact that she felt she couldn't talk to anybody about it. When you can't talk about things you don't understand, you become even more confused and upset.

"I was fat as a child. And when the woman next door was pregnant, I noticed her stomach was large. By then we'd been away from my grandparents for a year, but I didn't know anything about intercourse and pregnancy. The thought occurred to me that maybe I was pregnant since my stomach was large like this woman's. I can remember the terror I felt. I was afraid to go outside. I was afraid to have anyone look at me. I was almost immobilized by the fear and terror. But every day that I lived through it, it seemed as if I got less and less afraid."

What probably happened is that every day Amy "lived through it," her feelings became more and more frozen. This is what made survival more of a possibility. When a child so clearly talks about being afraid of having anyone look at her, and being afraid of going outside, it is almost a given that in adulthood her fear of going outside where others will see her will become even more painfully frightening.

Amy was an unwilling witness to her parents' sexual encounters, the victim of molestation by her grandfather, and totally lacking in any sort of healthy sex education. This made her the perfect victim.

Amy's parents' alcohol abuse continued to get worse.

"My father was seldom home evenings—he spent his time at the taverns. Weekends, especially Sundays, were eggshell days. We had to tiptoe around so as not to disturb my father. We didn't say much. We didn't do much. I think my brother and I learned this from my mother. She was emotionally afraid of my father, although he wasn't physically abusive to her or to us.

"Some Sundays we'd go for family drives. We'd pack sandwiches and drive to the lake. Mom and Dad would always be drinking. It would get dark, and my brother and I would be ready to go home. But my parents would both be pretty drunk by then, and sometimes they'd have sex on the beach in the dark, while my brother and I sat there waiting to go home."

Friday and Saturday nights, her parents went to the taverns to drink.

"When we were younger, my parents would take my brother and me along. He and I would sit in the family room at the tavern, eating while my parents drank."

Eating had obviously become a way for Amy to assuage the feelings that could not be expressed verbally. By fifth grade she weighed 145 pounds; by seventh grade, although she was only five feet tall, she weighed 185 pounds. Food may have medicated her feelings, but it also demonstrated how out of control she felt about her body. Eating became a way of masking her shame and the upsetting and confusing sexual development of her body.

The family moved a lot as Amy was growing up. They would often move because her father would find fault with his job or the town and decide to look for something better somewhere else.

This constant moving meant that Amy had to keep changing schools. However, she was a good student, and school seemed to be a safe haven for her, despite the fact that she was teased about her weight by the other students.

"School was escape for me. I made good grades. I could do well in class. But socially I was a loner. I had only one friend at a time, usually someone who was a misfit like me."

In many ways being loners protects children who move a lot. If they don't bond to other children, they don't feel the pain of separating. Also, if they don't bond, their "secrets" are less likely to come out. Unfortunately this life-style directly interferes with being able to bond with potential friends and love interests later on in life.

The summer Amy was eleven, her grandparents came for a visit.

"There was a racetrack nearby, and my grandfather asked me to go for a drive with him to the racetrack. I knew instantly what he wanted. But I knew that somehow I needed to go—and that this had to stop.

"There was no one at the racetrack, of course. I was sitting in the backseat. My grandfather stopped the car, turned around, and put his hand on my leg. He asked me why I didn't come sit with him in the front seat. I told him no. He asked me again to come sit in the front seat, and suddenly the words just came out of my mouth.

"I told him that if he ever touched me again, I would kill him. I was only eleven years old, but I meant what I said. I would try to kill him if he ever touched me again because it had to stop; I just couldn't take it anymore.

"He said, 'You don't really mean that, do you?'

"And I looked straight at him and said, 'Yes, I do.' He told me not to be that way. But I didn't say another word—I just sat there and looked at him.

"I guess he realized I was serious, because he turned around in the front seat of the car. No other words were spoken. He just drove me home, and he never ever touched me again."

Amy had found the strength and courage to say no. Saying no was fighting for her life. That "No, or I will kill you" was the outpouring of all the anger she'd been building up about the unfairness of her life.

Nevertheless, although Amy was able to stop the cycle of abuse by confronting her grandfather and saying no, irreversible damage had already been done. The combination of suffering the covert emotional sexual abuse of her parents and the overt physical sexual abuse of her grandfather left her feeling ashamed, dirty, and sexually confused.

"It was at about this time that I discovered masturbation. I felt very guilty about it, but it was a form of escape for me. I spent a lot of time doing it whenever I was alone and whenever I could."

Obsessive masturbation is common to incest and molestation survivors. It may offer solace, and it may also be a way of playing out conflicted feelings regarding the abuse.

Amy had also developed a fear of men, something that was not helped by the amount of time she spent in taverns, watching her parents drink. She found the loud, drunken men who hung out in those places very threatening. But she was powerless to do anything with those feelings.

"At this point, I had begun consciously to hate alcohol and the taverns. I just wanted to tear all the taverns down."

When she was fourteen the family moved to the country, and Amy began to attend high school.

"We were out in the country, and my brother and I would spend a lot of evenings alone. Dad would come

*home from work, get Mom, and they'd go to town and
drink.*

*"Long before I was old enough to get my driver's
license, I had become the reluctant chauffeur in the wee
hours of Sunday morning, after my parents had been
out drinking all day and most of the night. The car had
an automatic shift, and I'd drive very, very slowly. My
fingers and hands would hurt from gripping the steering
wheel so hard. My brother and I would be in the front
seat, careful never to look in the back because we never
knew what state of undress my mother and father might
be in. Sometimes we'd talk just to drown out the noises.
Sometimes my parents would be mad at each other, and
then it wouldn't be so bad."*

Amy began having trouble in school around her soph-
omore year. She had been used to getting mostly A's.
But now her grades dropped to B's and C's.

Up to this time, Amy had done a good job of compartmentalizing her life. How she presented herself in
public was very different from how she felt in private.
She appeared happy, confident, bright, and attractive to
others but felt terrified, insecure, and ugly. She had
learned well how to separate her feelings and attitudes
to portray to the world she was okay and to convince
herself she was okay. She was fighting to survive. COAs
and children who live with physical and sexual abuse
often become adept at compartmentalizing their feelings and perceptions of people.

The greater the trauma—and in this case there are
dual dynamics of both alcoholism and incest—the less
a child is capable of compartmentalizing for as long as

he or she may be able to if only responding to one dynamic.

"It was very difficult to go to school and concentrate. It just seemed like there was a gray fog that slipped down around my mind, and I couldn't concentrate anymore.

"My father never went to any of my school functions, and the one time my mother agreed to go, she was stark raving sober. Her hands shook continuously, and she was so horribly tense and irritable that I was ashamed of her and embarrassed. And then I'd feel guilty for being ashamed of her. I just felt that my mom wasn't like the other girls' moms, and I wasn't like the other girls. I felt we weren't as good, and I felt awful. I seldom went to school functions after that."

Amy spent her last years of high school managing the household. She prepared whatever meals were to be cooked and did all the cleaning and washing. The pressures on her were enormous,

"I was thin then, and I looked very good on the outside. But on the inside, I felt extremely crazy. There was nothing for me at that time to medicate the pain and fear. It was a very painful time for me, and I began to think about suicide."

During that time, in the middle of a fight with her mother and brother, Amy's father walked out of the house for good. He refused to give the family any support, and even though Amy's mother was working at a local restaurant, Amy had to buy her own food out of money from a part-time job.

That Christmas Amy's father showed up at the house. He and Amy's mother had been out drinking the night before, and when Amy got up Christmas morning, her father and mother were in the living room.

"They told my brother and me that they were thinking about getting back together, but that the decision was up to us. My father made it very clear that he would come home only if my brother and I would approve of it. I couldn't accept the responsibility for that decision. I told him that anything he and Mom decided was all right with me, but that it was their decision to make.

"My father left, my mother began crying, and I felt guilty. It was a no-win situation. But I also knew that if my father came back, nothing would change. It would be the same old arguments, but somehow my brother and I would then be responsible."

As many COAs do, Amy had acquired wisdom beyond her years. She could see the no-win situation she was in. She was skillful enough to try not to get caught in the middle, but she was correct about not being able to win. And, again, as many COAs do, in spite of all this wisdom, she found pregnancy and an early marriage the answer to her problems. Amy got pregnant just before she finished high school. She graduated in May and married Allen in September.

"I knew Allen drank a lot, but I thought that was normal for teenagers. He had already had a serious car accident because he'd been out drinking and had

smashed the car into a tree on the way home. It's amazing to me now that I never saw his drinking as alcoholism; I never saw what I was getting into. I thought I was getting out of something—that he would get me away from that alcoholic home. It seemed to me that he knew what he wanted, and he worked every day and didn't drink every day, so he seemed okay to me.''

Although Allen's alcohol abuse was blatant, what Amy didn't realize was that she was comparing his drinking with the later-stage chemical dependency of her parents. She had spent a number of years minimizing and denying. She'd been taught not to question. And then there was the clincher—Allen was her ticket out of the family.

CINDY
Age: 28
Mother: Alcoholic
Father: Sexual abuser
Other Abusers: Brother, brother's friends, strangers
Birth Order: Fifth of eight children
Raised: Northwest
Socioeconomic Status: Working class

CINDY: *"I had been in recovery for my alcoholism for four years, and I was doing a Fifth Step exercise. I was asked, 'Were you ever sexually abused?' I immediately answered, 'Yes.' Then I heard what I'd said and went into shock.*

"I had never thought of myself as sexually abused. But then I began to remember specific instances, although the memories weren't clear and I kept doubting whether any of it had happened or if I was just imagining it. I just didn't want it to be true."

Like many molestation and incest victims, Cindy had deeply suppressed the memory of the abuse. Not until adulthood does it resurface. Addiction and compulsive behaviors often help to keep memories suppressed.

But Cindy had begun a recovery process from an addiction.

As survivors give up their old defenses, their memories become more accessible. For some the memories come in dreams, for others in flashbacks, and at times— as it did for Cindy—as a spontaneous admission of factual memory.

As Laura Davis and Ellen Bass point out in their book, *The Courage to Heal,* remembering is the first step in healing. To begin the process one first has to remember that abuse actually occurred. Second come the memories of specific events. The third step in remembering is recovering one's feelings at the time the abuse took place. At this point Cindy has begun her recovery from sexual abuse.

Cindy's memories of her childhood are of her mother's drinking and her father treating her as his "special little girl."

"When I was young, my father wasn't violent as far as touching me. I was more Daddy's little girl. I went with him everywhere, even when he was meeting one of his lady friends. My mother was the practicing alcoholic,

and I was the youngest of three girls. It seemed as if my dad were trying to protect me more than the rest of my siblings. I felt really special, and he always told me I was really special to him."

This bonding was a major contributing factor in Cindy's denial that the parent she was most attached to had actively violated her. The conflict was so great that she'd had no other option but to repress the memories.

Cindy's memories of her mother revolve around alcohol.

"My mother was always busy drinking. She was drunk a lot. I remember she would hide the beer bottles in the cereal cabinet or below the sink. There was always lots of booze around. She was loud when she drank. She would fall down a lot on the floor or into the walls. I was always afraid of her. She looked so mean. If she got mad, she'd go for the belt.

"She did manage to take care of the household stuff. With ten in the family, it seemed as if she was always folding laundry. She was an excellent cook, and supper was always at six, when Dad came home."

Cindy's feelings for her mother were mostly based on how uncomfortable she felt around her.

"My mother always kept her distance from everyone. I don't remember her spending much time alone with just me or even playing with me. In fact, I don't ever remember her doing that.

"Mom got mad a lot, and I never knew what caused

it. She would yell, stomp around, and slam doors and cabinets really loudly.''

Cindy looked to her father for companionship and comfort. She needed attention and affection. All children do.

"The times my dad spent at home, I always tried to be with him. I don't think my mom liked that very much because I got most of his attention. I would go on errands with him, and he'd talk to me about the women he was seeing.

"One time, he took me to a small garage where he stored things. He had a mattress in there. He lay down on the mattress and told me I could sit down. I had no idea what was going on.

"Then a lady walked in. I'll never forget her. I couldn't stand her. She was mean, and she yelled at kids a lot. She kissed my dad and lay next to him and hugged him. My dad touched her all over, making lots of noises. I kept thinking, Why is my dad doing this with another woman?

"This happened a lot when I was very young, and eventually there were other women. On the way home from each of these encounters, Dad would tell me the story I was to tell Mom, because she'd always ask me lots of questions. It got to the point where I hated going with my dad on errands, so I'd hide when I knew he was going somewhere.''

This emotional incest eventually turned into physical incest.

"The farthest back I can remember it happening was when I was eight or nine years old. I used to wet my bed a lot, so sometimes my sister would wake me up and take me to the bathroom so she could change my bed. I was always a heavy sleeper, so I never knew if I was dreaming or awake.

"Did I really see my dad stooped down next to me with his fingers inside me while I was on the toilet? It felt like it. And it seemed weird that when my dad realized my eyes were open, he pulled his hands away from me and stood up quick. But I doubted my perceptions: first because dads didn't do that to daughters, and second because nothing was ever said, so I figured I'd dreamed it. I know now that it wasn't a dream."

Cindy cared for her father more deeply than her mother. She was more comfortable with him than her mother.

This again creates confusion for the survivor as the memories begin to surface. When a child chooses to spend time with a perpetrator, it is not for sex. The child doesn't want sex. The child wants to believe the parent is loving and good. Attention, hearing compliments, being held, are natural needs of a child. Generally the child is unable to avoid the offender(s) not just because (s)he may be an immediate family member, but also because the child is usually dependent on that person for daily needs.

The sexual abuse that Cindy experienced from her father was also carried on by her older brother.

"My father wasn't home very much. He was always away, 'taking care of business,' so my older brother

took over the father role. Unfortunately he did this in more ways than one. I always looked up to my brother. I was also very afraid of him. He was big and strong, and I'll never forget the look in his eyes when he was mad. Fear would shoot through me. I would freeze and then do whatever he told me to.

"One day, the house was pretty empty. I don't know where everyone was. My brother asked me to come into his bedroom, which wasn't uncommon; he spent a lot of time there. He was lying down on his bed, and he said he had something for me to do, but not to worry because all kids our age did this. I was ten then, and he was fourteen. He told me it would feel good.

"I remember being scared, but I didn't know what I was scared of. Then he pulled out his penis, and I thought my heart stopped. He told me to rub it and help him feel good. He said if I did that, then he would make me feel good, too.

"I didn't know what to do. The thought of telling someone never crossed my mind. So I did what he told me to do. Forty-five minutes later I walked out of the room and totally blocked out what had just happened. After that first time, this went on quite often—at least three or four times a week."

It is very common for a child who is sexually exploited to be abused by more than one offender. The offenders may or may not recognize this, but the victim certainly knows. Some Adult Children begin recognizing sexual abuse by one offender first, then realize it has also happened with others. They won't necessarily be able to identify all the offenders at once because of residual guilt, shame, and denial.

Sibling incest can be as traumatic as incest between a parent and a child. Clearly, Cindy saw her brother as a power figure, an authority to be feared. Terrified and confused, she did as she was told. With sibling incest the greater the age difference, the greater the betrayal of trust and the more violent the incest tends to be.

Adult survivors often minimize the incest by believing that all siblings are sexual with each other. "Playing doctor" represents normal sexual experimentation when the siblings are young, very close to the same age, have equal power with each other and in the family, where there is no coercion, and when the sexual play is the result of natural curiosity, exploration, and mutual sexual naiveté. None of that was true of Cindy's sexual abuse by her brother.

The patterns of sexual abuse continued on into Cindy's teens. By that point her brother began to give her drugs for having sex with him.

"My brother was really into drugs, and he drank a lot of beer. By the time I was in my early teens, he was giving me drugs and letting me party with him and his friends. At the time, I thought I was so lucky and special."

Cindy was getting her attention through sex, first from her father and then from her brother. But there were still times when she tried to stop her brother from abusing her.

"My parents worked at my grandparents' lumber supply store. We kids would go there on weekends to help out. There was a loft above the store, and I'd hide up

there whenever someone yelled at me, or sometimes I would just go up there to play.

"But the loft was also the place where I'd have to meet my brother. Sometimes I'd get brave and say I didn't want to do it. But then he would give me that look that said, 'You'd better do it or else!' I also knew that if I had sex with him, I'd get some of whatever he was dealing at the time."

As much as Cindy wanted the abuse to stop, by now her pain was so great and her sense of powerlessness so deep that she felt alcohol and drugs were her only answer.

Cindy's parents divorced when Cindy was fifteen. After her father moved, Cindy didn't see him much. When she did see him he always responded to her in a sexual way.

"He would greet me with, 'How's my sexy girl?' or, 'Hey, babe, you're looking good!' while eyeing me up and down. I'd laugh it off sometimes. Other times I wondered why he talked to me that way."

Cindy's father had given her the message over and over again that women were good for only one thing.

"He would talk about girls and how they were no good, filthy, worthless. He was always saying, 'All women are good for is housework and fucking,' 'Women get what they ask for—they ask to be hurt,' 'It's a woman's fault when she gets raped,' 'The man is the master of the house,' 'Women should be grateful to their men no mat-

ter how they're treated,' 'Women are pigs, and they smell.' ''

Cindy was doing a lot of drugs and drinking heavily on a daily basis by then. She also began to be promiscuous.

"I wanted so much for someone to like me, to love me. I started going out with guys when I was fourteen. Almost immediately, I was having sex with them. The first guy I had sex with was at a party. I always thought that there were two things I knew I could do well: one was to drink, and the other was to get a guy in bed. I thought these two things were points of pride."

Cindy dropped out of high school her junior year. She was most likely a young girl barely noticed at school and barely noticed when she was no longer in school. However, she looked old for her age and began hanging out at bars and having sex with strangers.

"There were bars where I could get in and drink for free. I'd leave with some guy I didn't even know. I remember many times waking up and not even knowing who I was with or where I was."

Sex was the only way Cindy knew how to get attention from men. She didn't know how to develop friendships with girls. And her behavior prevented many girls from seeking her friendship.

The men whom Cindy was having sex with were usually four to eight years older than she was. She would meet them at bars or at parties.

"I remember one incident when I was sixteen years old. I was seeing a twenty-four-year-old who lived with three or four other guys. He and I had gone to bed. Later that night, someone came into the bedroom, lay next to me, and asked if I'd been fucked yet. I said yes. Then he took his clothes off, grabbed me by the hair, and made me suck his penis. This went on for about an hour. I thought I was going to be sick. My whole body was trembling. I had tears in my eyes, but I was scared to say no. I was afraid that he would hurt me worse. When he finished with me, he just got up and left the room. All I could do was lie there, crying to myself. The next day, he just totally ignored me.

"These nights would happen to me a lot. They didn't seem as bad when I was drunk, though. I couldn't remember what had happened then."

Cindy's self-destructive behavior went beyond the sex, alcohol, and drugs. She had reached such a point of self-hate that she began to try to find other ways to hurt herself.

"I'd get high any way I could. Then I'd carve my skin with needles, pens, blades—anything sharp. I also ran away a lot. Once I almost drank myself to death with one-hundred-ninety-proof alcohol."

The physical pain that comes with self-mutilation may be a way of distracting oneself from the emotional pain. It may also have been an attempt on Cindy's part to draw attention to get help for herself. The sad thing is that no one paid any attention.

Cindy took to hitchhiking by herself.

"I was always picked up by guys, never women. There were times when carloads of guys would pick me up and not let me out until they all got what they wanted. Then they'd kick me out of the car and I'd put out my thumb again. Sometimes I'd get picked up by the same car two or three times in a row."

When she was seventeen Cindy became pregnant by an eighteen-year-old boy she met at a bar. He said he would marry her, but that it was now or never. Though she was skeptical of marriage, she took the now.

———————————

JOSH
Age: 31
Mother: Alcoholic, sexually abusive
Father: Alcoholic, physically violent, and abusive
Birth Order: Fourth of five boys
Raised: West Coast
Socioeconomic Status: Middle class

———————————

This story reflects the life in an alcoholic family that was affected by both physical and sexual abuse. Stories of sexual abuse most often reflect female abuse, especially female abuse by a male. This leaves male survivors feeling isolated—and male survivors molested by females even more isolated. Josh's story is about mother-son abuse. It is also my observation that male incest occurs more frequently in alcoholic families when both parents are alcoholic, as in Josh's situation.

Josh's father was a violent drunk who would abuse both his wife and his sons.

JOSH: *"I remember hiding in the closet with my brother when my dad started beating up my mother. I was only five or six at the time. I remember asking my mother why she stayed with a man who beat her up. She would respond that she loved him, or say, 'He's your father. Don't talk about him that way.' "*

It was about this same time that the sexual abuse began. Josh's mother would get drunk and molest him. He was seven the first time it happened.

"I'd stay home with my mother on Friday and Saturday nights, listening to her tell stories of her childhood. She'd drink one drink after another, and begin talking about how women were different from men. Then she'd do a striptease and tell me to touch her. After that, she'd lead me to the bedroom, where the incest would take place. I was so confused. I felt lost. I had seen my mother and father have intercourse many times, but I'd never had her direct her sexuality at me. I was also terrified that if my dad found out, he would kill me.

"I can clearly remember the first time. I was so scared and so confused, it felt as if my whole nervous system was on fire. I started to cut out during the experience. There was this splitting, this separation, and I was no longer in my body. It was as if I went to a new dimension. And I remained there until it was over and I came out of a fog."

The splitting Josh refers to is a common way for children to deal with the experience of being abused. Most survivors experience it to some degree. They describe it as living in the mental level; being in one's thoughts; not being fully present; leaving one's body; a sensation of floating above oneself; or doing as Josh did, going somewhere he can't identify, a different dimension. Splitting is a very understandable defense. These children cannot run away physically, so they emotionally and/or mentally leave their bodies.

Josh's feelings about the sexual abuse were also compounded by his fear of his father's homicidal rages. Very often he would endanger the children's lives.

"Once when I was seven, my father went into one of his rages and ordered my older brother and me to go out and stand in the street so he could run us over with the car. He physically threw us into the street, got in the car, and started driving straight for us. Luckily, we jumped out of his way in time. He even stopped and tried to back up, but we ran and hid in the woods. I never knew what we did that was so bad."

The message is so innocently clear to Josh, or to any child whose life is threatened by a parent: they are so bad, they must be killed. The child believes the parent must be right; after all, they are adults, and they know everything.

Josh was sexually abused by his mother until he was nearly twelve. She used the ploy that she was teaching him how to be a good lover and how to make a woman feel good. The incest included fondling, oral sex, masturbation, and penetration on two occasions.

In addition to his mother's molestation, Josh was forced to witness his parents' sexual behavior.

"They would have intercourse in front of us children at all hours. One time we were all in the car and they actually stopped the car and had us get out, and they had intercourse along the side of the road."

Experiencing a parent's nudity is humiliating and a covert form of sexual abuse—sexual abuse without the touch.

"My dad was always naked. He would eat naked. It was never safe to bring someone home. I always had to check and see if he had his pants on. Then I would take my friends to my room because I didn't know what they would see outside of my room.

"My dad was obsessed with the size of the penises of all of us boys. He would always make crude comments about our sexual prowess. We never had any pajamas or robes until we were older, and then we bought them for ourselves."

Taunting sexual comments and focusing on penis size is also sexual abuse without touch. It is very destructive to a child's healthy sexual development and self-worth.

To add to the confusion and sense of insanity, Josh's father would always try to put on a good face in front of the neighbors.

"One time, my father was chasing me around the house next door, trying to catch me. He stopped in the midst of his pursuit to wave hello to the neighbors who were sitting on their porch at the time. Then he continued to chase me until I tried to run into our house. He caught my leg in the door and kept me pinned there while he kept smashing my leg with the door and screaming, 'I'm

going to kill you!' The reason for this rage was that I had accidentally broken a light bulb in the garage.''

It is so difficult to imagine children living like this. Their lives are terrifying and crazy making. Children like Josh cannot make sense out of why they're forced to live as they do, so they actively respond to their life in the best way they can. By the time Josh was in the second grade, he had begun running away from home on a periodic basis. If he couldn't find a friends' home to stay at, he would stay out late.

"I didn't think I'd be missed. I'd go to a friend's house; I hoped that maybe his family would want to keep me for a while. But his parents would always call my parents to let them know I was okay. But at least I'd get to spend the night at my friend's.''

At some level, Josh knew he deserved better. At times he'd go shopping for new parents.

"I would go to the parents of my friends and literally interview them. I would ask them about their house rules. I would ask whether or not they spanked their children. I wanted to know about allowances.''

Josh needed someone to help him, someone to do it for him. He couldn't extricate himself from this family all by himself. At this young age, if someone had tried, it might have been possible. But within a few years he was so hooked psychologically, he couldn't leave even when he was legally able to do so. Josh summarizes it well.

"We were just five little boys all trying to raise ourselves."

Josh began drinking by the time he was ten.

"I drank to cover up the fear that seemed to follow me around. I didn't drink a lot at that time, but somehow I felt as if all this craziness was my fault. The drinking helped me forget the fear and my sense of guilt."

When Josh was thirteen, he began to notice that his mother was very sick.

"She was turning yellow, and I kept telling everyone she was sick. They all told me I was seeing things. It wasn't until my grandmother came to visit that my mother was taken to the doctor. The doctor said she had cirrhosis of the liver and put her in the hospital."

The hospitalization did nothing to stop her drinking, though.

"When I would go to visit her, she would beg me to bring her beer. My dad told me to do it, so I did. She got worse and worse, and they even tried experimental surgery on her, but nothing worked. I remember my father walking into her room, drunk, and asking her where she wanted to be buried. I began to cry, and my father grabbed me and shook me, saying, 'There's no reason to cry. That's the way things are.' "

Josh's mother would spend two years in and out of hospitals.

"In my own mind, the first time my mother went into the hospital is when she died. After that time she was always changed. Looking back now, I believe she had become psychotic—probably an alcoholic psychosis."

It was at the time of his mother's first hospitalization that Josh began to use Valium.

"I began to take Valium to help me cope with the stress and violence in my life. By the time I was fourteen I was addicted to it. I managed to control my use during school hours, probably out of fear of getting caught. But I would abuse it at night and on weekends."

Josh also became sexually active at a very young age, which is often true of incest victims. By the third grade he would engage girls in petting and kissing. By the fourth grade he was having dates in which he was going to the movies with girls and engaging in sexual behavior more typical of an adolescent. He was never forceful with girls. After all, his mother had taught him about pleasing girls. She had also told him, "If you ever hit or hurt a woman, I will shoot you."

At fifteen Josh got a job at a gas station in order to support himself, going home only to sleep. However, his employers found out that he was underage, and he lost the job.

"By the time I was sixteen, I frequently suffered from depression and thoughts of suicide. I had a girlfriend at the time who acted like a mother for me. She helped me go on even though there were times when I didn't want to."

This girlfriend probably saved Josh's life. She became a tenuous lifeline for him. Most Adult Children can look back and identify one or two people who made enough of a difference to keep them from becoming overwhelmed by rage or depression or from taking the final step and committing suicide.

When Josh was seventeen, however, he did attempt suicide.

"I just couldn't handle the pain and grief any longer, so I tried to overdose on pills. Luckily a friend stopped by unexpectedly. He worked in a hospital emergency room, so he did all the right things to keep me alive. When I woke up twelve hours later in the hospital, my friend was sitting right there."

After Josh graduated from high school, he went on to nursing school. But he continued to live at home even though his parents' drinking, his father's rages, and his mother's insanity grew worse.

Despite how traumatic life has been for them, many COAs don't leave home once they're legally of age or out of school. Often they stay in the home because they have little money and because they lack the needed social and emotional support to leave. Many don't leave out of fear of what might happen if they did. They believe their physical presence protects others in the home. This was true for Josh.

"I stayed at home to protect my mother. I was there to help her. I needed to protect her, to fix things. If I didn't, I felt she would literally die."

Special Issues for the Sexually Abused ACOA

DON'T TALK

One of the most difficult issues facing children who have been sexually abused is the alcoholic family's "Don't talk" rule. The children have already learned this negative admonition regarding the alcoholism in the family.

"Don't talk" carries with it an inappropriate sense of loyalty. By talking, the child is somehow betraying the family's secret. If the child does talk, especially to another family member, the child usually comes up against a wall of denial: "That never happened." "Your father would never do that!" After hearing that over and over, telling others quickly ceases to be an option. Children intuitively believe that others do not want to know and/or would not believe them. As Cindy says:

"I was the one who was always wrong."

Incest victims and COAs succumb to a powerlessness, a learned helplessness. By not talking, they discover that things are more peaceful at home. In fact, talking often worsens the situation. To suffer the abuse is degrading, humiliating, violating. Not to be believed only intensifies the trauma.

This denial, plus being betrayed by someone you love, can be extremely debilitating for abused children since they are already confused about what has happened to them. In the case of incest, a trusted family member is the offender. And this person then tells them that they must never tell anyone, that they must keep the secret. There may be threats of family separation or even death if the truth is told. This closes off their hope of stopping the abuse—the intervention of another adult.

Amy learned the "Don't talk" rule in relation to her parents' alcoholism.

AMY: *"As the alcoholism progressed in my family, the family got more and more silent and the house got more and more silent. We withdrew from each other. It got to the point where we really didn't talk to each other about much of anything. We couldn't even talk about 'safe' things, such as a TV program. How could we ever talk about the things we knew weren't safe?"*

Because the pattern of denial and silence had already been established in her family, Amy naturally extended that to the fact that her grandfather was molesting her. She didn't believe that telling anyone what was going on was even an option. The situation was made all the worse by the fact that there was no clear model for her about what was and what was not acceptable behavior.

"I had no model for what was healthy and normal. I had never been taught that if someone treated you badly or did something to you that was wrong, you had a choice of telling that person no. I had no inner resources to rely on to tell me what was not acceptable. My reaction was to think there must be something wrong with me."

Amy was also monetarily rewarded for her silence. This isn't what kept her silent, but it made the situation even more complex.

Amy's grandfather paid for her silence by giving her

money each time he had sex with her. He was essentially rewarding her for "not talking." She used the money to buy food to "stuff" her feelings. Keeping the secret adds to the hopeless cycle.

Amy's grandfather gave her money, and Cindy's brother gave her drugs. Both girls were being bought off to help keep the secret. When abused children keep the payoff, that adds to their later guilt of thinking they complied and it gets interpreted as their being at fault for the incest. It is significant to note that both of these girls quickly got rid of their payoff—used the drugs, bought food. In both cases the payoffs offered medication.

Somehow, though, Amy did find the resources within herself to confront her offender. Although she was unable to talk to anyone else about the abuse until she was in recovery, at least she was able to break the silence by saying no to her grandfather when she was eleven.

Cindy had learned the "Don't talk" rule from her mother before the incest began.

CINDY: *"I was so afraid of my mom as a little kid. We could never do anything right. So I stayed outside and tried to not draw attention to myself. To be safe I would hide in closets and in the cabinets in the bathroom. I would also get behind drapes close to the heat register and lie still. At times Mom would lock us out, and I would huddle by the heat vent from the dryer to stay warm."*

The "Don't talk" rule isn't just about secrets. Cindy was learning not to talk about anything—talk of any kind was not safe. When abuse became a part of her life, she was already programmed to be silent.

The "Don't talk" message in Cindy's family was reinforced by threats. Cindy's brother and father both had violent tempers that terrorized her into silence and compliance. What made things worse was that it never occurred to her to tell anyone. Besides, whom could she tell?

Her mother had already abandoned her through her use of alcohol. Cindy was totally unable to perceive people outside the family as potential sources of help. And even if she had, what would she tell? She had so deeply denied her father's abuse that it wasn't until recovery that she began to realize that what she had experienced was real, not made up.

The pattern of denial was also very strong in Josh's household. No one talked about what was going on, and every attempt on Josh's part to identify the problem was rebuffed.

JOSH: "I learned not to trust my perceptions of what was going on. And the message not to talk about them openly came through loud and clear. What I learned was a warped version of 'What you see and what you hear, when you leave, you leave it here.' I believed that if I told anybody what I felt, my mom would find out and then she wouldn't like me, or even worse, she would tell my father. I knew what he would do if he found out. By that time, I had seen enough black eyes and bruises to assume that would be the price to pay.

"I knew that, no matter what, I was never to tell anybody anything."

POWERLESSNESS

Adult Children have learned to feel powerless. They have no control over their parents' alcoholism. And they are powerless to stop it.

AMY: *"I was watching my parents die a day at a time, but I was powerless to do anything about it. I also equated powerlessness with being good. I learned at both church and school that good children were obedient. Being good meant doing what you were told. Taking power was not a 'good' thing."*

Children are so hungry for love and approval that inappropriate attention can easily confuse them. This is why they're so easily victimized. The needier they are, the more vulnerable they are, the more easily they fall prey to abuse.

Amy felt that food was the one thing she had some control over. Each time she sneaked food or went out and bought herself some candy or a banana split, she was trying to regain some of the power and control she felt she had lost.

AMY: *"The money gave me a sense of control, a sense of power. By spending the money to buy food, which I was using to anesthetize my pain and anger, I felt I was gaining the power not to have my food controlled."*

Cindy had learned at a young age that her body was not her own. She learned that her father and brother had power over her body, and that she had no control over what they did to her. The few times as a teenager that she tried to stand up to her brother, he would threaten her and once again she would become power-less.

Cindy's sense of powerlessness was carried over into her relationships with other men. They were able to abuse her body and treat her horribly, and she never had the sense that she had any power to stop it.

CINDY: *"When I was around guys I always felt 'less than.' My shame would overwhelm me: my head would drop down, my body would shrivel, and I couldn't stand up straight. They didn't even have to say anything, their presence was enough to bring on a shame attack."*

Cindy came to believe that her only value was in being used sexually.

Josh grew up feeling powerless to stop his father's physical abuse of himself, his brothers, and his mother. The only way to deal with it was to run, either physically or emotionally.

JOSH: *"I can remember hearing my mother begging my father to stop hitting her. I felt so powerless, I wanted to die. One time my brother and I confronted him and told him, 'Don't you hit her again!' But he just beat her more when we weren't there.*

"I was also afraid that if I hit him, I wouldn't be able to stop. I was certain I would kill him. I was powerless to hit him because I believed my rage was so murderous."

As a child Josh would run, duck, or hide to avoid the beatings. He also learned to stay away from home, to avoid both his father's beatings and his mother's sexual abuse.

"I would leave the house a lot. Sometimes I'd go sleep in the woods and let nature take care of me. I just wanted to go to the woods and lie down. I couldn't handle what was happening at home."

As he grew older, Josh used alcohol and drugs as a way of hiding. Drugs and booze helped him forget his lack of control over his life.

The powerlessness that children feel in the hands of their abusers is overwhelming. Children in alcoholic families know nothing about healthy boundaries. No one has ever told them that their bodies are their own, or that they have the power to say no. They feel that the abuse is something they have to endure, something they are powerless to stop. Because they are children, they lack both the physical and the psychological power to protect themselves.

When abuse continues into adolescence, and the teen finally has the physical power to fight or run, this learned helplessness often keeps the young person in the victim role.

FEAR, GUILT, AND SHAME

Adult Children have learned to "stuff" their feelings. They have learned that it's not okay to cry. It's not okay to get angry. It's not okay to ask for help when you're afraid. The feelings of fear, guilt, and shame that permeate the life of the abused child must be shut down, locked away, or channeled toward less threatening targets.

AMY: *"My parents' alcoholism and the accompanying poverty set up an atmosphere of fear, shame, and guilt. There was so much pain that I was forever seeking ways to escape it. I found food, fantasy, reading, and television. I was always looking for someplace safe. But I never did feel safe. And I never felt good about myself or even adequate. No matter what my successes or achievements, I never felt adequate. I was never enough."*

Amy felt anger both toward her parents for their drinking and inappropriate sexual behavior and toward her grandfather for molesting her. But she had no safe place to release that anger.

"Anger was just not expressed in my home—particularly when my father was home. Feelings were not acceptable. Nobody talked about feelings, and that was the message I got about anger. Women and children were never to get angry at men. If you got angry at Dad, he might leave.

"The underlying feeling was that if he left, you would die. The internal message I got from the shame and guilt and fear I felt because of the molestation was that I didn't have the right to be angry about anything. I always envied my brother's ability to express anger. He was the acting-out child. I just kept my anger locked up inside me."

The fear Amy felt about her abuse manifested itself in other ways.

"For a while when I was nearly twelve I suffered from agoraphobia. I was afraid to go out on the streets alone,

to go to the grocery store for my mother, or anywhere else. I had an overwhelming terror of all men. I was afraid to look at the men I passed on the streets. I was afraid that they were looking at me. It was very painful. Whenever I was out I would feel sick. Finally, because I had no choice about going to school and having to go out, I simply became more and more numb.''

Agoraphobia, the fear of open spaces, is common to both COAs and incest survivors. Amy's agoraphobia was precipitated by feelings of fear, of not being safe. Her menstrual cycle had just begun, and her family had just moved physically nearer her grandfather. Her fear was immobilizing.

"Early on, I tried not to feel the pain, not to feel the fear, not to feel anything. The problem was that along with trying not to feel those negative, destructive feelings, I was also not allowing myself to feel the positive, joyful feelings and experiences that might have been there for me. I did not allow myself to reach out to others who might have been able to be there emotionally for me. I was trying to protect myself in order to survive. But in doing so, I missed a lot of the good things I might have had in my life. I lost my ability to identify my feelings, to express them. I had become emotionally numb.''

Cindy also learned to freeze her feelings.

CINDY: *"I came into this world not feeling safe. The first feelings I can ever recall were fear and not being*

*wanted. I always felt as if I had somehow ruined my
mother's life. She would tell me that I was a trouble-
maker. The message I got was that I wasn't worth anything. If your mother doesn't want you, then you must
not be wanted by anyone. I soon learned to freeze my
feelings. They were too painful to deal with.*

*"Every time my father would spew out his hatred of
women, I felt as if it were directed right at me. I would
feel small, no good, filthy, worthless. I hated him when
he talked that way, and he did it all the time. I'd get
very angry, but I knew if I told him I was angry, he'd
just yell louder—and he might even start hitting me. So
I kept everything inside."*

The fear that Cindy experienced with her father and
her brother was later extended to other men.

*"I still get scared thinking about how it felt to be forced
to have sex. My body shakes, and my legs hurt. I close
or cross my legs because I feel pressure in my vagina.
I hate it. God, I hate it.*

*"There were times when I'd be tied up, gagged, or
hit. I learned to cry quietly, if at all. I would blank out
or drift off as if I weren't there. I felt dead."*

Cindy believed she was responsible for the sexual
abuse, that she was somehow to blame. And because
she blamed herself, she felt guilty and ashamed.

*"I couldn't tell anybody what had happened to me. I
felt too dirty and ashamed to admit it. All I wanted was
love from someone. When I was a little girl, I'd crawl
up onto my father's lap or lie next to him on the floor,*

and he'd pay some attention to me. That's why the strange touches didn't seem so bad. At least he noticed me.

"When my parents divorced, even though I outwardly blamed my mother, I thought I was the cause of their breakup. But then my father hardly ever called me, and he stopped spending any time with me. I couldn't understand it. I thought I was special to him. He had always told me how much he loved me and that he would always be there and never leave me. I figured I must have done something wrong to make him abandon me."

Cindy's confusion is so painful. The one person she feels some closeness to is one of her primary abusers. He is the only one who has ever given her any sense of worth; yet not only does he violate her himself, he does nothing to protect her or to stop the abuse by her brother or the men she meets at bars. Her need for her father's love and approval comes from such a vast emptiness.

Cindy's shame was so great that she felt it was something wrong in her that made men have sex with her and then abandon her.

"I was so mixed up. I kept trying to figure out what I was doing wrong that made these guys use me and then go away. Why didn't they like me unless I slept with them? I couldn't figure it out. Why wouldn't anyone love me?"

Feelings were never safe for Cindy. She would live out a pattern of self-destruction and self-loathing.

Josh learned from an early age not to trust his feelings or perceptions.

JOSH: *"I learned, growing up, that it's no good to cry. I wasn't to cry when my father tried to kill me or hurt me. I wasn't to cry when I felt sadness for my mother. The message was that my feelings were not okay, and that I was not okay."*

The sexual abuse that Josh suffered as a young boy added to his sense of shame and low self-esteem. He felt responsible for what had happened to him.

"I needed love and attention from my mom, but then she'd go into this striptease and molest me. I wanted her to stop, but I didn't know how. I felt so powerless. But I'd always understood that men had more power than women—that was very clear to me from the way my father treated my mother. I'd learned very graphically by the time I was five that he was always on top and she was always on the bottom.

"I thought I should have known what to do, how to get myself out of this situation. I should have been a grown-up and done the right thing. I had this terrible sense of shame because I didn't know what to do. I didn't know how to extricate myself from the pain.

"There was so much pain. My body hurt physically from beatings and emotionally from the craziness of my life. I was so confused sexually. I felt cheap, dirty, and totally ashamed. I was afraid of both my mother and my father. I felt guilty, as if I deserved their abuse."

These feelings of shame and inadequacy often lead incest survivors to self-destruction or compulsive behavior, which is an attempt to mask the shame. Amy resorted first to food, and then to compulsive masturbation. Cindy used alcohol, drugs, promiscuity, and razor blades for self-mutilation. Josh used alcohol and Valium. He also experienced anorexia. Although this eating disorder is more common among women, it is also prevalent among incest victims.

"Those times when I felt the greatest powerlessness, when I felt least in control in my life, I would stop eating and work compulsively. I would find a hundred things to do in two hours and do them all. If that didn't work, I'd drive around, just to keep moving."

Life for these children is a constant internal struggle. Living in an alcoholic or sexually abusing home is traumatic in and of itself. But when both occur together, the child needs to construct even greater defenses. However, these defenses don't usually stay intact as long as those of other Adult Children. Their inner child and physical being are just too tired. The pain begins to show itself quickly.

Life Stories: Adulthood and Recovery

AMY
Age: 48
Partner Status: Married, three children
Occupation: Office manager, insurance firm
Recovery Process: Al-Anon, OA, ACOA, AA, nine
   years sober

Amy was pregnant when she got married, and her son was born just before Christmas. She was very sick after he was born, and she and the baby spent their first New Year's Eve alone.

AMY: *"My husband went out by himself and got drunk. I can remember my sadness and the sinking feeling I had at the time. It was like a blow. I felt dazed. But I internalized the feelings. It was something I'd just have to accept. That was the way it was, there was really no escape, and it probably wasn't going to get any better."*

Amy had had years of practice in "accepting the intolerable," but she had deluded herself into thinking that her escape into marriage would make her life different and better. Within six months of her marriage, when she was only eighteen, she knew on some level that life was going to remain the same. This time she had no fight left, and she responded by spiraling into greater powerlessness.

Amy soon began to suffer from various illnesses, such as bronchitis, strep throat, and colitis. These can all be symptoms of the "silently enraged." As an ACOA, incest victim, and the wife of an alcoholic, Amy had many things to be angry about, but no self-worth or skills to deal with that anger effectively.

"During the early years of our marriage, it seemed as though the pain was acute all the time. I suffered from severe depression. It was all I could do to cook the meals and get the laundry done. I was also doing a lot of eating. I had gained forty or fifty pounds when I was

pregnant the first time, and I never took it off. I continued to eat just to keep going.''

Amy became pregnant again the following year. Her mother had been evicted from her apartment and came to stay with Amy and her husband.

"She said she needed help and had no place else to go. She said she just couldn't go on, so my husband and I took her to the doctor and then committed her to the state mental hospital. Then my brother came to live with us. He was sleeping on the floor of the kitchen, but after two months my husband finally contacted my dad and said he had to take my brother to live with him."

After Amy's mother got out of the hospital, she came to stay with Amy again.

"She was with us only a week before she started going downtown during the day and coming home drunk. I was very angry with her and just wanted her to go away. I couldn't take it anymore. She finally got a job and moved out."

Two weeks before Amy's second son was born, her husband had to have emergency surgery. With the family pressures, her husband's and her own illnesses, and her constant state of depression, Amy began to drink to relieve the pain.

"In the beginning, I drank to escape. It was the very best escape I'd found so far. It was also the most powerful. I didn't have that knot in my gut anymore. Al-

cohol seemed to transform me. I could begin to express my feelings. But I was also very afraid of drinking because I'd seen what alcohol had done to my parents."

Despite what Amy had seen with her parents, her attraction to alcohol soon became greater than her fear. Without any recourse to internal resources and skills, alcohol and food were Amy's only answers to her pain.

Amy combined eating binges with her drinking.

"I still continued to eat a lot during that time, and my diet consisted mostly of refined sugars and starches. I was getting both my alcohol fix and my sugar fix. But then my eating and drinking binges started getting closer and closer together. I was completely losing control."

Amy's husband was also drinking a great deal.

"When we were first married, my husband was kind of attentive. He seemed to be interested in me and what was happening with me. But then it was as if he changed overnight. He suddenly ceased to be affectionate. The few times I tried to approach him emotionally, he rejected me, so I learned not to take that risk. Coming out of the alcoholic background of my family, it was like a door had closed. I felt that this was the way it was going to be for the rest of my life and that I just had to learn to live with it. I felt no particular sense of loss or grief—it was just a matter of 'Don't think about it and go on. Just make the best of it.' "

Amy's third child was a daughter. Six months later, when Amy was twenty-one, she attempted suicide with pills.

For the next twenty years Amy continued to abuse alcohol and food. She was in an emotionally distant relationship, and she was depressed and suicidal. Finally she ran out of ways to try to hide from her pain.

"By now my husband and I were having drinking wars. I was so tired. I felt as if I'd been fighting my entire life. I had a friend who had gone to Al-Anon, and I had seen the change in her. I decided to try Al-Anon myself—I was totally oblivious to the fact that I was alcoholic.

"However, I believe that, for me, it was important to go to Al-Anon first. What Al-Anon did for me was to help me begin to address some of my resentments about my parents' alcoholism. In the meetings, some of the pain began to dissipate—just enough to begin the healing process.

"I had been carrying this big bag of pain loaded with fear, guilt, and shame all of my life, and it was in Al-Anon that I began to lighten the load a little bit at a time, without adding to it. I began to have hope for the first time in my life—hope that maybe I didn't have to continue the way I was. Hope that maybe things could be better for me.

"Once that started happening, I finally had to face my own drinking. I no longer had any rational excuse to drink. Yet I'd still find myself getting drunk occasionally, and I absolutely could not understand that. Finally, I had to face the fact that I was an alcoholic, that I was addicted to alcohol.

"Even though I was afraid of everything and every-

body, including myself, I somehow found the courage to go to AA. At the meetings, for the first time in my life, I had a sense of 'This is what a real family feels like. This is what home feels like.' ''

Even though Amy had good feelings about finding a home, she had trouble learning to trust other people enough to open up and share.

"I think it was the fear that I would have to live my life drinking that kept me coming back. I had no other place to go. I didn't know how to get rid of my resentments, my anger, my fear of not being able to stay sober.

"My first two and a half years in AA was a very confusing time for me. About all I could hold on to was the fellowship and the feelings I had while I was at the meetings. I seemed unable to carry the information I got at the meetings outside and apply it to my life. The Twelve Steps meant nothing; they just didn't compute.

"I just kept trying, kept reading, and kept making an attempt to pray every now and then. I was very angry with my husband because he refused to go to meetings with me. He told me I was definitely not an alcoholic and that he wasn't going to any meetings or marriage counselors. I was very hurt and angry about that. I was envious of the people in AA and Al-Anon who had spouses who were participating, so I stopped going to Al-Anon.''

Amy had also been attending Overeaters Anonymous meetings, but at this point she stopped attending them, too, and began bingeing again.

"I was just returning to one of my addictions. I wasn't drinking, but I was using other chemicals—refined sugar and starch."

Finally her self-destructiveness culminated in leaving AA. As Amy gradually quit using her support systems, her anger with her husband began to surface.

"I felt haunted by my husband during that period, as though I didn't have a moment to myself, that I didn't belong to myself anymore. He was always invading my space, demanding my constant attention. Now, I can see clearly that he was abusing me emotionally.

"On the days when he was the most abusive, he wanted sex. But I was trying to sort through my own issues regarding my molestation. My husband made me feel as if something was wrong with me, that I must be frigid because I didn't want to go to bed with him. I just wanted to get away from him, to escape somehow. But the more I pulled away, the more determined he became. It became a power struggle, a war."

Amy now realizes that her husband felt threatened by her recovery; that he felt his own alcoholism was being attacked. His actions were motivated by fear. His obsession with sex was just another addiction for him and a way to be abusive toward her.

Amy was trying to deal with her husband, her worries about the family's financial stability, and the knowledge that her children were suffering from the battles that were going on in the family. Three months after her last AA meeting, Amy went on a three-day drunk that scared her into facing what was going on.

"I went back to AA with the knowledge that it was time to get honest. I finally surrendered. I believe that this is when my real recovery began.

I had to get in touch with my Higher Power, but it was very difficult for me. I was afraid of God. I felt that God was very punishing. I had to find the proper words to pray. But I could no longer live with a God that I was afraid of. I needed to have a God that I could pray to for anything in this world and truly believe that He would not give me anything that would harm me. I had a lot of old ideas about God that I needed to get rid of.

"The first thing I had to do was allow myself to feel the anger. It was very powerful for me to do that. It was also very healing. I had to realize that I was angry at whatever Higher Power that allowed me to be sexually abused by my grandfather. I could not believe that a loving God could have allowed that.

"I finally came to realize that it wasn't God's will that I should be molested—it was a misuse of my grandfather's free will. My grandfather was a very sick man— maybe he'd been powerless to do anything else.

"The bottom line was that God had nothing to do with it. God did not will it. God did not wish it. If my grandfather had been able to listen to his Higher Power while it was going on, I believe that he would have heard God saying to him, 'Please don't do this!' And I believe that my Higher Power cried during those times, probably weeping for both of us."

Although some alcoholics find it best to put off their Adult Child or incest work until they have been sober for some length of time, Amy needed to address her incest very quickly. Now that she was no longer abusing food and alcohol, all her rage had surfaced. It was imperative for her to face that rage in order to be able to integrate the principles and teachings of the AA program.

Amy first heard about the concept of Adult Children of Alcoholics at an AA meeting. After that, things began to click. She realized that she had to look at the whole picture of her family in order to make progress in her own recovery.

"To me, my alcoholism is all one piece. Growing up in an alcoholic home is not a separate issue from my drinking or eating. To me, alcoholism involves all of oneself—physical, mental, emotional, and spiritual. And I'd already had the mental, emotional, and spiritual illness before I began drinking. All it took was the addition of the alcohol for the physical symptoms of that illness to manifest.

"The resentment and anger I had about my grandfather haunted me in recovery. I became very aware that I needed to get rid of that resentment, to come to terms with it and find some peace. I made an attempt to pray for my grandfather, even though he has been dead for years. But after trying for a long time, I just realized I couldn't do it. I had to be honest with God about that. I told God that I knew that my grandfather was one of His children, and that I knew in my heart that he was very sick. But I had to own my honest feelings. I hoped my grandfather burned in hell for what he'd done to me. Not just for the physical abuse, but for all the emotional pain, the losses that I suffered over the years because of him, my inability to get close to a

*man emotionally and sexually—all the destruction it
caused in my life.*

*"I admitted to God that I could not forgive my grand-
father, that I could not have any good feelings about
him, that I truly hated him for what he'd done to me. I
asked God to go in my place and do that which I could
not do for myself—forgive my grandfather. I asked God
to do that for me."*

Many Adult Children and incest survivors want to
forgive their abusers before they have fully owned the
depth of their own experiences. I don't think it is possible to forgive if you haven't walked through your anger and rage first. It is possible to come to an intellectual
understanding—but not to truly forgive.

When Amy realized that she couldn't forgive, but that
her God was able to do what she could not, she found
the freedom to let go of some of her anger and resentment. Eventually she found the strength to talk about
the molestation at one of her meetings. The feedback
she received, especially from some other members who
were dealing with their own abuse issues, was very validating.

Many incest survivors need to participate in a same-
sex group. An all-women's or all-men's group can offer
great comfort and support. Ultimately, however, incest
survivors will heal even more so when they allow themselves to participate in a group experience where the
focus is on incest.

Amy had reasons to be angry at her parents for not
protecting her from her grandfather and for their openly
displayed sexual behavior. She found she needed to
speak to that anger as well.

"I have written a lot of letters to my family that were not mailed. I read the letters out loud to other recovering Adult Children and then destroyed the letters.

"My next step was to work on anger toward myself. I needed to forgive myself for not telling anyone what was happening to me. I had to understand why and forgive myself for that."

Letter writing is a technique many Adult Children have found helpful in their healing process. They write a letter to a particular person. It is a letter not to be mailed, shown, or read to the person it's directed toward (unless it's a letter to oneself). But it is a letter that the Adult Child will very likely read out loud to a therapist or other recovering person. The focus of the letters may vary, but in general the letters to a family member(s) express experiences, feelings, and needs that were neglected—so much of what has never been safe to acknowledge. It's an emotionally cathartic healing process that offers the Adult Child greater clarity about feelings and needs of the past and present.

Intertwined with the issue of anger, Amy is facing the role of abandonment in her life.

"Sometimes it seems as if I was abandoned emotionally. But other times it feels as if I was never claimed in the first place. It's as if the adults around me were unable to acknowledge me. It always felt as if something had been taken away, as if my parents had walked away from me or left me alone.

"Looking back on it, I realize that because I couldn't express the pain, the shame, and the anger that I felt when I was a child, I had abandoned myself. I'd had

no other choice. In order to survive, I had to walk away. I had to abandon that child, abandon those feelings as best I could.

"Part of the struggle in my recovery is to reverse that process. Now I need to reclaim the child I walked away from so long ago. There's so much healing in that. Sometimes I feel so sad for that little girl. And sometimes I'm just amazed that I managed to survive it all, and that I'm doing as well as I am.

"I have also come to realize that what my grandfather did to me was not about sex; it was about power. It's an abuse issue that has more to do with self-esteem. I realize I have no reason to feel guilty about what happened. I know now that my body belongs to me and to God. Who I allow to touch me, who I allow to get close to me, is between God and me. It's my choice. And no one else's. There is a great deal of freedom in that. In recognizing that I do have choices, I've come a long way."

CINDY
Age: 28
Partner Status: Married, two sons
Occupation: Computer programmer
Recovery Process: AA, six years sober; Adult Child
  therapy

Cindy was eighteen when she had her first child. Fifteen months later she had her second child. She says that her attitude was that it didn't matter if she got pregnant, while at the same time she believed magically that it wouldn't happen. And when it did happen she was totally unprepared.

CINDY: *"I spent a lot of time at home with my first child. My husband worked during the day and spent the nights until closing time in bars. By the time my second baby arrived, I was going out more. I left my kids with my sisters or my mother-in-law. I can clearly remember holding my second baby when he was an infant and my husband, Tom, and I playing Pass Out, drinking gallons of booze.*

"We moved a lot in those years. We lived with relatives a lot of the time. I'd often leave the kids alone when they were asleep. Or I'd leave them with my mom, knowing she'd pass out early. I was an absolutely terrible parent. I yelled at them a lot. I didn't want them. One time I wanted to punish Tom, so I moved out and left the kids with him."

When Cindy and her husband were twenty-three and twenty-four, respectively, they decided to go for alcoholism treatment. Cindy has no memory of why or how they decided to seek help. She's not even sure if it was a joint decision. She clearly remembers looking at herself in the mirror one day and seeing her mother.

"I have no memory of calling for help or where my husband fit in. We separated and got back together that first year, and we've both stayed sober. It has been six years now."

All during these years Cindy's father was continuing his inappropriate sexual behavior whenever he was around.

"My dad didn't stop touching me. He'd grab my rear or come up behind me and lean against me, putting his hands on my legs and rubbing them, telling me how I was 'filling out.' I kept thinking, Fathers don't do this to their daughters, do they?"

Cindy was still so overcome with powerlessness around men that she clearly presented herself as a person who would not fight back or protest. She was a prime victim. And like most Adult Children, she still wanted her father's attention. She'd had so few healthy people in her life to offer a sense of normalcy, or self-respect, that many of her old patterns continued.

Then Cindy began to reject her husband whenever he tried to touch her.

"I was so scared of being touched by anyone. I'd freeze when my husband came near me. It wasn't just him, either. I couldn't even stand to have one of my women friends touch me. I was aware of how paralyzed I was. But I didn't know what was happening to me. I thought I liked to be around people, but here I was, trying to isolate myself. I couldn't believe this was happening to me. But no matter how much I isolated myself physically from other people, I still couldn't tell my dad to stop."

Memories of incest first came to Cindy when she was sharing her Fifth Step of Alcoholics Anonymous. The heart of the AA program is found in the Twelve Steps (see appendix 1, page 161). In the Fourth Step one takes a searching and fearless moral inventory. The Fifth Step is sharing that inventory with another human being and your Higher Power. It was in this process that Cindy was confronted with more truth of her past.

"Finally I had to face the fact of the sexual abuse in my life. At first I told myself, 'Well, it wasn't so bad. This sort of thing happens in all families.' I thought it was normal. I had trouble even saying the words sexual abuse. I kept referring to it as 'this' or 'that.' Naming it made it more real, and I didn't want it to be real. I was afraid I wouldn't be able to handle going through the remembering, that it would be too much. But I was also so full of hurt and shame that I didn't want to admit it to anyone else."

Cindy's recovery was stymied. She was clean and sober and proud of it. But she was also so flooded with self-hate, rage, and fear that she was dying inside. She struggled painfully for several months, but her attraction to recovery was the strongest pull. She began to attend an Adult Child therapy group.

In her ACOA group, Cindy found that other people were telling her over and over that what she had experienced was emotionally, physically, sexually, and spiritually abusive.

"I was in a horrible dilemma. The more I remembered, the more I tried to block what few memories I had. But the more I tried to forget, the more I would remember. My body would shake. I wanted to spend all my time in the shower. I felt so dirty, as if something or someone

were on me and wouldn't get off. My paranoia about other people was completely out of control. I thought everybody was looking at me. I thought they all saw me as dirty. I knew I had to go back and try to work this out or I'd just end up using again and feeling totally crazy.

"In the end, I chose to live through it again. But this time I wasn't going to do it alone. I knew I had to tell my scary, shame-filled secret to someone."

It was this that finally led Cindy to ask for help. Someone suggested that she see a sex therapist.

"The therapist helped me separate my own stuff from what had gone on with my dad, my brothers, and the other men in my life. She taught me about my own body. I learned the difference between good touch and bad touch. She validated many of my fears and helped me understand that I'd had good reason to be afraid."

Through her work with the therapist and in ACOA, Cindy began to get in touch with some of the feelings that she had locked away.

"The abuse was probably the hardest, scariest issue I had to deal with. I prayed for strength all the time. I still do. Initially I was even angry that I had to see the therapist. I told myself that if I hadn't been abused as a kid, I wouldn't be in so much pain now. There were many times when I thought of giving up and putting it all in the back of my mind. I even thought of taking my life. Thank God I didn't."

Cindy's struggle is common to the recovery process. Many people who were sexually abused would like to take a big eraser and "make it all go away." That is the role alcohol, drugs, and promiscuous sexual behavior served for Cindy. The truth is, no matter how hard you try, it won't go away. Attempts to deny or forget just prolong the pain. As painful as facing the truth is, it is the only way out of the cycle of abuse and all the hurtful consequences that occurred with it. Truth is the only protection from denial and deception. It will mean freedom and choice. Cindy was willing to trust that.

"But in my heart of hearts I knew I couldn't forget anymore. I finally made the commitment to look at the abuse instead of denying it. It was reality. I couldn't pretend that being abused hadn't affected my adulthood. My marriage had been at risk many times. We would fight and argue. But instead of trying to work it out, I'd go find another man.

"That had always helped me forget my pain before, why not now? But I knew that running from reality was no longer an option.

"I have lived with fear all of my life. What I began to learn is that letting go of that fear required a deep sense of trust. It required surrendering to God, to my Higher Power. That was really hard. How do you trust something you've never seen or touched or felt, especially when everyone you have seen or touched or felt has damaged you?"

You learn to trust slowly. You learn to trust by allowing others to be a part of the process. Cindy's continuing recovery from her addictions is what helped her at this point. She used what she had learned in that recovery to empower herself to take further risks.

"The memories were actually physically painful. At times I thought I would die. I kept thinking about self-mutilation. I kept thinking about getting wasted on drugs and alcohol. Yet somehow I believed I could and would get through this. So I let myself be with the pain. I knew I had no control over this, but I also knew I wasn't alone—and it wasn't an earthly being. Whatever I'd glimpsed of a Higher Power in my work in AA was with me. I came through. I came through with a stronger connection to my Higher Power and to myself. I am no longer willing to believe that I am at fault, or bad."

One of the most difficult issues for Cindy was confronting the reality of her past and then confronting the people who had hurt her.

"I was afraid of confrontation. Confrontation meant you would get shamed or hit, or you'd run into denial. I was also afraid to confront the shame, guilt, anger, and sadness I had."

But it was so important to Cindy to find out what others knew that she tried talking to various members of her family. She asked her sisters if they remembered any abuse. They said that they did remember their father treating Cindy differently and making sexual remarks to her. But then they discounted that by saying, "That was just Dad. You know the way he is." Cindy didn't even get that much acknowledgment from her mother or brothers. And when she confronted the abusing brother, he told her that they hadn't done anything that all brothers and sisters didn't do. Only recently has one brother actually listened to her without discounting her perceptions.

Very often Adult Children and incest survivors receive no validation or support from family members. When they open the subject, they are often made to feel "wrong" or "bad" for saying such things.

Whether or not to confront family members is a decision all recovering incest survivors have to make. Confronting abusers or family members is not necessary for the healing of all survivors. It's an individual process and an individual decision.

What is important is knowing your motives. Many survivors want to discuss it with family members to gather facts from others. This was what motivated Cindy. You may want family members to validate your perceptions that these things occurred. You may want to break the silence. You may want others to know so they'll be more empathetic to who you are. You may want revenge. It's important to know your motives. If you know why you want to confront the family, you are able to look at your desire more realistically and as a result will be more likely to get your needs met.

Many incest survivors have confronted family members, shared with nonabusive family members, and felt good about the process. Others only feel greater rejection. In consideration of talking with family members, talk with others who've had similar experiences. Share your hopes and expectations, and strategize what you want to say. On the other hand, other incest survivors have chosen not to talk to family members and have felt very satisfied with their ability to move on in recovery.

Cindy was still having problems confronting her father, though.

"My dad's behavior toward me hadn't stopped. Whenever he came around, he would talk about past affairs he'd had and how many times he could make women come, as if I was supposed to be impressed. I felt like throwing up on him. I was scared to be around my own father.

"My dad would still touch me and make gross, sick comments about me. I was trying really hard to stay with myself and not allow him to abuse me. But it's so scary and so hard."

Finally Cindy put a stop to the cycle of abuse. She decided that, for now, she wouldn't confront her father about what had happened in her childhood—but that she would stop his present abuse.

"I can finally say that my father no longer has control over me. I will not allow him to abuse me any longer. For the time being, I won't see him or talk to him.

"I feel like killing him, and I'm glad I'm angry. It's about time. I never thought it was okay for me to express my anger because if I did, I wouldn't be liked or people would leave me. But my friends have shown me that they won't leave me if I feel anger. I had to trust them and have faith that they would stay. I was scared to trust, but they have stayed.

"I now know that I no longer have to carry my father's pain. I'm done being 'loyal' to him—and loyal I was.

I'm not responsible for his actions. I can be free of him. I can now work on being a mother to my own children and a wife to my husband.

"Today, I'm beginning to learn how to deal with my feelings of helplessness. I'm discovering that even if I can't change a situation, I do have options in the way I choose to respond to things. I do have power because I always have choices.

"When I think about how long I was abused, it makes me cry. I get very sad and scared. But I know I have the choice whether or not it continues. I thank God for my friends, my husband, and my children. But most of all, I thank God that I'm finally, finally able to love myself enough to say No!

"I am a miracle. And I thank God for the blessing of being allowed to see myself as a miracle."

JOSH
Age: 31
Partner Status: Divorced
Occupation: Physical therapist
Recovery Process: AA, six years sober; Adult Child
   therapy

After graduating from high school, Josh remained at home and attended nursing school. While he was in the nursing program, he was finally forced to confront his father's violence.

JOSH: *"It was a subzero night in January. I had just started nursing school, and I was working at our local hospital. I'd just finished a forty-eight-hour shift. There was a blizzard, and I had an accident on the way home. I had to contact my father to get information about our insurance, which meant I had to call six or seven bars before I found him. He was furious over the phone, and I was scared to go home, but I was so exhausted I went home anyway.*

"When I walked in, my father was standing in the kitchen, naked as usual, except he was holding a shotgun. I just froze, not knowing whether to run or to stand and face him. I stood there for what seemed like an hour. I knew he was drunk. Then he started yelling about how I'd always cost him money, how I'd ruined his life. He then picked up the shotgun and aimed it at me.

"I was afraid of dying, but I was tired, really tired. I turned my back on him, saying, 'If you shoot me, you're not going to get away with it.' I heard him scream, and then he began hitting me with the butt of the gun. Somehow I managed to get away and slept in the car."

The next day Josh fell asleep during a nursing exam. He realized that he was unable to function, so he went to talk to the director of the program. At first he was afraid to tell anybody the truth; he was afraid no one would believe him. However, once he did open up to the director, she took him to see the school counselor, who got him into a psychiatric hospital for three months.

"They diagnosed me as depressed with hysterical tendencies. I underwent hypnosis, along with sodium pentothal treatments. I attempted suicide again. I just

wanted to be crazy and not have to go home. My parents never came to visit, just my girlfriend."

Josh was even willing to be crazy if that meant not having to go back home and keep living as he had been all of his life. He had no answers, no solutions. The system he was seeking help from kept enabling his belief that "he was the problem." Many do not escape being institutionalized repetitively, but fortunately Josh discovered that he was not crazy and that he found no value in being perceived as crazy. After three months he returned home. However, having to deal with his father sent him right back to using drugs.

"From the first word my father spoke to me when I got home, my own disease worsened. For the next seven years I drank and used as often as I could."

During this period, Josh married a woman who was also an Adult Child. Neither one was in recovery at that time, and within two years the marriage ended in divorce. By now Josh had left nursing school, but he was studying to be a physical therapist.

Soon he was in a relationship with a woman who had been court-ordered into treatment for her alcohol and drug abuse for traffic violations. In going to see a counselor with her—to help "fix" her—Josh was confronted with his usage. He openly admitted he was alcoholic. With that, he began to participate in Alcoholics Anonymous. It was as if he'd been ready and waiting, as if he'd just needed the correct opportunity. Unfortunately, after thirty days sober, he relapsed. And in that relapse he made his last suicide attempt.

Josh had used various means of attempting suicide over the years. One time he used pills; another time he tried to slash his wrist with a knife; this time he lay down in the middle of a major highway, hoping someone would run over him. Later he commented wryly, *"I wasn't even good at committing suicide!"*

While Josh was in a psychiatric hospital because of his last suicide attempt, a very astute nurse counselor suggested he seek co-dependency treatment.

"There was a therapist there, a dynamite lady, who taught me that I wasn't crazy, which was what I'd always assumed until then. She saw something in me that I wasn't able to see—an intuitive ability to help others who suffered the way I did. She told me: 'Josh, you're bright, and you give great feedback. But when are you going to be important enough to yourself to focus on you?' That statement changed my life. With the help of God, I didn't leave treatment."

After he was released from the hospital, Josh went back to Alcoholics Anonymous and also began attending Adult Children of Alcoholics self-help meetings. He is continuing in both programs.

"I had to do both programs at the same time because I was in so much pain. I had too much rage inside me to stay sober, so I had to let some of the rage go. This is what I was able to do with my Adult Child work. I also needed it to help me separate from my family. What I had to learn immediately was how to establish boundaries and how to take care of me. I couldn't have stayed sober without this."

The ability to set limits is vital to feeling good about oneself. Survivors and Adult Children are not skilled at defining their time, at protecting their bodies, or at putting themselves first. Amy, Cindy, and Josh all had to learn how to set limits and establish boundaries in order to recover. When they did begin to set limits with their family members, they were protecting themselves and freeing themselves at the same time. When we can protect ourselves from situations we don't want to be in, we experience confidence, power, and self-respect.

"With the help of my therapist, I have begun to change my old patterns of behavior and to stop being a victim. I got involved with a grief therapist. I had so many grief issues. I felt as if I'd been dead all of my life. I have had to grieve for the childhood I never had. I have had to do rage work around specific instances of sexual and physical abuse. I needed to learn healthy ways in which to physically respond to my abuse. I found I needed to scream, and I needed to hit—for that I have used battacas [heavily padded sticks] and pillows. Therapy gave me a safe and secure environment in which to do that.

"Allowing myself the rage was so scary. I always felt that if I got in touch with my rage, I'd be just like my father. This made me so fearful of my rage that I stayed a victim. By getting in touch with my rage I have been able to free my inner child. I have been able to let go of so much pain. I also found out I am not like my dad. I don't have to hurt myself or anyone else when I'm angry. Before, I couldn't get past the rage to feel anything else. But letting go of my rage has made it possible for me to get in touch with all my feelings. I can now separate anger out as its own feeling as well.

"Getting in touch with the rage was freeing and exhilarating, but it's only one chunk of my healing. Nevertheless, it's been a vital chunk, and it has made it possible for me to love myself."

Adult children and incest survivors have many times found it helpful to physically release their feelings of rage. In order to feel safe with the intensity of their feelings, this is best done with a therapist with whom you have a trusting relationship. Psychodramatic and Gestalt therapy techniques are more frequently used, where you confront an object or other person who symbolizes your parent(s) and speak that which has not been previously safe to say. With the use of pillows, battacas, possibly tennis rackets—any object that can be held but is nonhurtful—you can physically respond with your anger. Although not all incest survivors or Adult Children have found this necessary, many have found it very helpful. For Josh, it was very freeing.

It is easy to see the similarities between Josh's experiences and those of the two women. The effects of abuse are equally profound whether the victim is male or female. Yet, while they have much in common, it has been less acceptable culturally for men to show any feeling but anger. As a result, men express their pain differently from women. Very early on, male and female children are given messages about feelings that are specific to their gender. They learn that it's okay for girls to cry, as they are viewed as the weaker sex. However, boys cannot cry, but they may assert their anger. They are told that, aside from anger, feelings are weak, feelings are feminine, and it's not okay to be feminine.

Because of these cultural messages, male incest survivors spend a great deal of time trying to think their way out of feelings rather than feeling them. This is complicated further by being raised in a home that is both alcoholic and incestuous. It means that even greater pain will have to be discounted and repressed in order to survive.

Josh needed to get in touch with his rage, as did Amy and Cindy. But as a male, it is even more important that his rage not be a reenactment of the one feeling males are allowed. Michael Lew, author of *Victims No Longer*, says: "In their attempts to counteract feelings of vulnerability and impaired masculinity, adult male survivors can end up feeling that their only protection lies in intimidating the world with a theatrical display of anger."

Josh's work around anger was not about intimidation, because he was not protecting his vulnerability. Josh's anger was a form of indignation over the injustices he'd suffered. He was also able to feel his sadness and fear and his tremendous sense of loss. He is learning to get in touch with his entire range of feelings.

"My life is by no means perfect. I married another ACOA after I was two years sober, and that didn't work out, either. However, I have learned some valuable lessons. I realized that by choosing women who were non-recovering ACOAs or addicts, I was still trying to fix my mom and bond with her. My mother has only gotten worse over the years, and it still hurts that I can't do anything about it. But today I know that I do have choices about how I live my life.

"I see my father about twice a year now. He's still

drinking, but I no longer allow him to be a threat to my existence. Today, one of my brothers is six months sober, and my younger brother has been involved in Adult Child recovery for the last six months. I'm no longer the only one in my family in recovery.

"My life is fuller than it's ever been. The people I have in my life today are there because of my healthy choices, not because I was limited to the attitudes I grew up with. I now help other Adult Children learn to make their own choices. I help them understand and deal with the trauma of growing up with people who are addicted."

Amy, Cindy, and Josh would have faced the hardship of "double duty" simply by the fact that each had two alcoholic parents. But adding the incest complicated the issues exponentially. Their need to protect themselves has been so much greater that it has led to a severe splitting off from their emotional selves. Greater shame and self-blame leads to more severe depression, alcoholism, and drug abuse at a younger age. And this, in turn, leads to eating disorders, thoughts of suicide, and suicide attempts.

Yet all three are in recovery today. Cindy and Josh needed to become clean and sober first before it was safe to address these issues. Amy, on the other hand, had to begin acknowledging the incest and her rage about it before she could get sober. Once they were no longer medicated and anesthetized, all three discovered that their lives would be severely limited until they addressed both their Adult Child issues—and the incest. Because of their experiences in AA, they had begun to trust the process of talking.

Hopefully, the experiences of these people will help incest survivors who have not had any previous experience with self-help groups feel safer and more trusting about reaching out to a resource.

Recovery Considerations

The stories we've shared throughout this book, and particularly in this chapter, are testaments to the inner strength and survival capacities of children. Being incest survivors in chemically dependent families creates "Double Duty/Dual Identities." For many this often means triple, even quadruple duty.

The trauma these people have experienced has been profound, and in recovery it is imperative that they address both issues. Which one should be addressed first is usually clear, because you identify first with either the incest or the alcoholism, and that dictates how you reach out for help.

Many Adult Children don't remember the incest until they begin their ACOA recovery. As you begin to let go of repressed thinking and controlled behaviors, you will begin to feel more and more. As you become more trusting of others, memories will often begin to surface.

That is what occurred for Cindy. She had been in recovery from her alcoholism a few years. She was feeling safe—not needing to protect herself as much—and suddenly the memory was there.

Other Adult Children seek counseling because they begin to experience flashbacks or a flood of memories of sexual abuse. Many people seek help not because they have identified either the family alcoholism or the incest, but because of depression, difficulties in relationships, or compulsive behaviors and addictions.

USING RESOURCES

In my experience, both Adult Child and incest survivor issues need to be and can be addressed simultaneously. Many Adult Children work on the incest with a therapist while also attending ACOA self-help groups. Or they attend Incest Survivors Anonymous and ACOA or a similar combination. Because not all ACOAs are incest survivors, if your recovery is primarily in ACOA groups, it is important for you to have an opportunity to meet in a setting where the focus is on incest.

It may be feasible and desirable to have both individual therapy and a group experience at the same time. Should you be too frightened to join any group—either a self-help group or a therapy group—you may want to begin your recovery with an individual counselor. It may be necessary for you to work one on one for a time before you feel ready for a group experience.

But be aware that group opportunities are there, both for therapy and for self-help, and that both are extremely valuable. Talking with others who have had the same experiences as you is extremely validating and supportive. You deserve that. Other group members will not reject you. They will understand, believe, and support you.

Above all, because life was so unsafe for so many years, your own personal sense of safety must be your first priority. There is no right way and wrong way here. Know that you are free to begin your recovery with the process that appeals to you most and feels the safest.

Adult Children and survivors also find comfort, direction, and hope in reading materials. There are many books on the healing of incest survivors. In fact, there are more books on this topic than on any other issue covered in this book (see bibliography, pages 179–182).

The thoughts below may offer you some directions to consider in your recovery.

UNDOING DENIAL

Truth is the only protection from denial. It is denial that has kept us shamebound. It is truth that will lead us to recovery. This in turn creates, or maintains us in unhealthy relationships, compulsive behavior, and/or addictions. It is shame that keeps us immobilized and depressed. Although we were victimized as children, we do not deserve to continue to live our lives as victims. We are survivors. As traumatic as the experiences were—we survived.

It is important to allow yourself to remember the past so that you can separate yourself from the abuser and from the internalized shame. You will need to talk about the experiences so that you can put them into perspective. In your childhood you saw these events through the eyes of a vulnerable child. This child believed that you must have deserved what you got, that you were bad. As an adult it is safer to speak to the injustice and the unfairness and the terror that were a part of the experiences.

However, it is important to speak the truth so that you can receive validation for your experiences. The validation was not there when you were a child. You deserve to know that your perceptions were correct. You may not get this from family members, but it can come from others familiar with abuse issues.

Not talking about it is a form of minimizing and denying the experience. It is a way of continuing to negate and deny yourself. The truth is the only way out of the cycle of abuse. The opportunity for validation is only one of the reasons the group experience is so important in recovery.

As you begin to speak your own truths, you might also want to carry the following truths in your heart:

• It was not your fault.
• You are not bad.
• You need to break the silence.
• You must not do this alone.

ANGER AND RAGE

It is healthy and necessary for incest survivors to grieve for the losses of their childhood. There was so much fear, humiliation, hurt, sadness, and confusion, and all of that needs to be talked about. But, ultimately, you must address your anger and rage. Josh makes this point so well when he says that until he was able to speak about his rage, he couldn't let go of his victim role. His fear of becoming enraged and hurtful to others kept him immobilized.

It is understandable that Adult Children would feel tremendous power in their rage and be fearful of that power. Yet survivors may be equating abuse and power. From experience, survivors learned that to be powerful one must be angry and hurtful toward others. But you need not be hurtful with your rage. There are many ways to open up to all of your feelings without harming anyone else or yourself. And once you do, you will experience a freeing of your pain that allows you to create a healthy framework for expressing your internal power.

Anger is part of the healing process of all Adult Children. Victims and survivors are either totally detached from, extremely frightened of, or overwhelmed by this feeling. If you don't feel anger, ask yourself "Where did it go? Why isn't it safe?" Be open to the fact that it is there—it just may not be very visible. Often, people have to confront their rage before they can separate out anger and any other feelings. People who are abused—and who are unable to focus their rage at the abuser—take their rage elsewhere. It can become an addiction or show up as compulsive behavior such as workaholism, perfectionism, compulsive masturbation, eating disorders, critical self-talk, chronic illness, or self-mutilation. You do not deserve to be rageful with yourself. This rage turned inward is really personal violence. It is okay to be angry. It is not okay to be violent with oneself or with others.

Directing your rage—not necessarily literally—at the abuser(s) and those who didn't protect you is pivotal to recovery. That rage can be directed toward the perpetrator(s) either face to face or symbolically. Many survivors find that physical releases of anger are helpful, such as hitting inanimate objects with a battaca or tennis racket; throwing objects into a safe place; or yelling. Experiential forms of therapy such as bioenergetics, psychodrama, and Gestalt are often helpful. As rage is released, it becomes easier to identify many feelings. Rage has been the holding tank for fear, sadness, and pain. Recovery means learning to explore and accept the entire range of human feeling.

Both Adult Children and incest survivors learn early

on to be internal controllers. And because they learn to control all their feelings and to dismiss all their needs so well, when they do begin to feel, they may also feel out of control.

Giving up internal control and feeling is contrary to what you've done for years in order to survive. Chances are, when we believe we're roaring, we're still only letting out a peep. To us, expressing any truth, any feeling, is so foreign that it is overwhelmingly frightening. Yet the more frightened you are of your rage, the greater safety you will feel in letting it out in a therapeutic context with the help of a professional who is familiar with Adult Children and incest survivors.

Remember, anger is a universal human experience. We all have it. Anger is a normal emotional response when someone hurts or wrongs you. It is not to be confused with blame. Blaming is anger that moves in circles, not directed out and released. Releasing our anger constructively allows us to work through the problem. Releasing anger gives us freedom. When anger is released in an honest, direct, constructive manner, it dissipates.

Recognizing anger also allows us to identify our needs. Anger is a natural response to exploitation, and it can be used as a cue for setting limits and boundaries. Anger is an important cue for self-care.

POWERLESSNESS

It is essential in recovery to recognize how little power you had as a child and to grieve over the trauma of being victimized. It is also vital to identify the ways you attempted to acquire power to overcome your terrible sense of loss. For some it was in fantasy, for others it was by hiding, for still others it was by eating or by starving.

An important aspect of recovery is to claim the power you do have today. You are no longer the child who was victimized. You are an adult who was once abused and once raised in an alcoholic family. You can go back and retrieve all the power you didn't have then. You do that by challenging the internalized messages that you learned to believe. You need to sit down and make a list of the messages you internalized about yourself— messages such as:

• You aren't worth anything.
• You'll never amount to anything.
• No one will ever believe you.
• You are stupid.
• You are bad.
• You aren't trustworthy.

Once you have made your list, you need to toss out those messages that you don't want to continue to incorporate into your life today and create new messages in their place. You can change these messages to:

• I am of value.
• I am important.
• I speak the truth.
• People will believe me.
• My perceptions are accurate.
• I am bright, capable, trustworthy.

Then you need to repeat those messages on a daily basis to yourself. Say them over and over until you feel them in your heart and believe them. Obviously, many feelings will arise as you do this. It's all part of the grief process. These are feelings that need to be identified and acknowledged. Just be patient—yet persistent.

Another way of reclaiming power is by establishing healthy boundaries. By setting limits and boundaries, you are protecting yourself. When we are taught to be the object of another person's prerogatives, to put another person's wants and desires first, we usually have to acknowledge the pain associated with having lived that way before we can set limits for ourselves. Along with that pain comes much sadness and much anger. Once the grief work has begun, it is easier to say: "I need. I want. I deserve." You will also find it easier to establish boundaries and limits in those areas where your needs and wants have to be protected and addressed.

By establishing boundaries and setting limits, the Adult Child survivor begins to use the words *No* and *Yes* with freedom. That also takes much work. It was not safe to say *No* as a child. Without the freedom to say *No*, *Yes* was said with tremendous fear and helplessness or out of a desperate need for approval and love.

Recovery means talking about the many times you couldn't say *No* but wanted to, and the anger and pain that goes with that. Recovery means seeing the ability to say *No* as a friend to protect you. It offers you choice. You have the power and right to say *No* and *Yes*. You will find that *Yes* is a gift that is offered freely rather than out of fear or the need for approval. Recognize that by saying *No*, you are actually saying *Yes* to your-

self. Just as important, you also have the right not to
say *Yes* or *No* until you know what it is that you want.

RECLAIMING RIGHTS

As children from troubled families, so many of our
rights were neglected and/or taken away. It is important
to go back and reclaim that which was rightfully ours
in childhood. This is an aspect of reparenting that is
vital in recovery. It is important that the following rights
be integrated into your hearts and minds because of the
incest you have experienced:

- You have the right to choose who can and who cannot touch you.
- You have the right to distinguish how you are
  touched and for how long. You have the right to
  determine what type of touch is acceptable to you.
- You have the right to say *No*.
- Not only are these your rights—they are rights you
  deserve.

TOLERANCE OF INAPPROPRIATE BEHAVIOR

Adult Children who are incest survivors lived for so
many years with chemically induced abusive behavior
that it began to seem normal to them. As a result, adult
survivors are not skilled at recognizing people's intrusive, disrespectful, and/or abusive behavior.

A part of recovery is learning to identify the inappropriate behavior you experienced in the past in order
to be free to identify it today. If you still minimize or
deny the unacceptable behavior of the past, you won't
have the skills to recognize it in the present. Learning
to identify behavior that was inappropriate in the past,

coupled with acknowledging and trusting your feelings, will make it much easier to recognize inappropriate behavior in the present. Add the belief that you deserve respect, and you can begin to set limits. Does this seem like an impossible task? No. It's very possible, and you can do it.

FORGIVENESS

As a group, Adult Children in general are desirous of understanding their parents' behavior. They are quick to bypass anger and jump into forgiveness. This has more to do with their fear of anger and need for approval than their desire to forgive.

Before forgiveness is truly possible, you must reclaim your emotional experience. By doing this, you also reclaim your power—without this, forgiveness will not occur.

Yet seeking to forgive your offender is not a necessary part of your recovery. Focus on your life—not what you believe you should or should not feel about the abuser. In your grief work, and in reclaiming your own life, you may come to find that you have less and less anger with the abuser. In time you may have only a distant sense of sadness, a remnant of anger. Clearly, an important goal in recovery is to have your anger with the offender no longer interfere with how you care about yourself or how you live your life. But it is unrealistic to expect yourself never to be angry again with the offender for the molestation.

Some people get confused about forgiveness, particularly when they realize that their parents were also abused as children. Although that information is helpful, and can put your family experiences into perspective, it does not erase the violations you experienced.

Remember, should you forgive, while you no longer blame the offender you do still hold the offender accountable for his or her actions. And you can and must continue to set limits when you are around that person. Forgiveness does not mean having a flash of insight and then resuming the old family roles.

Many people want to forgive themselves for things they did to others when they were children, often in response to having been hurt themselves. You may have physically hurt a smaller or younger child, or an animal. You may have molested a younger or smaller child, or, as Josh did, you may have initiated sex with other children. In the process of forgiving yourself, I hope that you will find compassion for your own vulnerability. Please try to remember that you were just a child. In *The Right to Innocence,* Beverly Engel reminds her readers that:

- You were a confused, disturbed child or adolescent acting out your pain.
- You were sexualized too early—long before you were emotionally and physically able to handle it.
- You had not yet developed a moral code, which is true of all children.
- You are different from the perpetrator because you are trying to change so you won't hurt anyone like that again.
- Just as you are not a bad person because of what someone else did to you, you are also not bad because of any sexual or cruel acts you committed as

a child as a consequence of the abuse you sustained.

On the other hand, if you believe you were old enough—probably sixteen or older—to be held accountable for your actions, and if you believe you acted freely, knowingly, and of your own accord, you may be suffering from healthy guilt. You will then need to learn from your actions so you do not repeat them.

Ask yourself, "Why was this a mistake?" "What were some of the other consequences?"

Find a way to atone for what you have done. Be accountable for your actions.

Seeking to forgive oneself means developing an empathy for how vulnerable you were as a child. Remember that forgiveness is a cleansing of your pain. You were just a child with the resources of a child.

CHEMICAL DEPENDENCY

Because so many abuse survivors become chemically dependent—which is even more likely when they are Children of Alcoholics—you should be open to questioning your own chemical use. Before you can recover effectively from your Adult Child survivorship issues, you must address your own possible dependency. You cannot heal from childhood sexual abuse if you are addicted to alcohol or drugs.

If it is possible to reach out for help regarding your ACOA and survivorship issues, but not chemical dependency, then go ahead and begin where you can. Just be aware that, in time, you will need to look at the role alcohol and other drugs play in your life.

REPEATING THE ABUSE

Without recovery, victims of physical and sexual abuse may become either abusers themselves or silent partners to their children's abuse. Both alcoholism and abuse are generational. It's almost unheard of to find only one abuser and one victim in any abused family. But the chain can be broken when people take action not to repeat the pattern. If you recognize this behavior in yourself, or you are fearful of it occurring, reach out and ask for help now! You can and must stop any abuse. You do not have to abuse or be a silent partner to the abuse of your children. There are people who can and will help. While there are specific resources listed in the appendix (see pages 175–176), help can also be found through your local crisis line, family service agencies, and rape crisis centers.

RELATIONSHIPS

Adult Children and incest survivors frequently have difficulty in relationships and understandably so. When one is Double Duty/Dual Identity, the reasons for this difficulty become even more complex.

Yet healthy relationships are possible. If you aren't in a relationship, you can learn a lot about intimacy in the context of a close friendship. Remember, as you recover specifically from ACOA/Incest issues, you are developing a more complete sense of yourself. And this is the basis of your strength in any relationship.

Work on knowing what you are feeling. You aren't going to be able to identify the relationship's needs if you don't know what your own feelings are. Being in a healthy relationship means acknowledging your own needs and feelings. It also means maintaining healthy personal boundaries so you can distinguish whose needs and feelings are whose and who is responsible for them.

Learning autonomy, knowing what you want, what you feel, what you need, and what you believe, allows you to develop as a unique entity, separate from others. Adult Children survivors are so often enmeshed with others that their personal self-worth is dependent upon making people feel good and important, on making other people happy, on seeing that other people's needs are met. You have to have a sense of yourself that is separate from others before you can have the healthy relationship you want.

In all relationships there is a need to learn healthy negotiation and conflict resolution. There was no model for this in the families of most COAs or incest survivors. Fear of anger and the need for approval are two Adult Child characteristics that clearly sabotage healthy negotiation and conflict resolution. You can only perceive options when you know your power. Conflict resolution is only possible when you have a healthy basis from which you can say *No* or *Yes* to your partner.

If you are in a relationship while you are working on these issues, this process will change and challenge your partnership. This can be very stressful. But if both of you are committed to growing, it can lead to greater health and happiness.

The courage it took to survive incest, and to survive incest in an alcoholic family, is cause for great celebration. Although recovery can seem an overwhelming task, when we are willing to allow others to walk through the process with us, we will see the darkness fade from our lives. We will find the freedom and happiness that we have always deserved, but that was postponed. May you find your happiness today.

I am no longer willing to believe that I am at fault or bad.

—*Adult Child Incest Survivor*

Notes

1. *Los Angeles Times* survey, August 1985.
2. H. Giaretto, *Child Abuse and Neglect* 6:3 (1982).
3. D. Russell, *The Secret Trauma: Incest in the Lives of Girls and Women* (New York: Basic Books, 1986).
4. C. Black, S. Bucky, and S. Padilla, "The Interpersonal and Emotional Consequences of Being an Adult Child of an Alcoholic," *Journal of International Addictions* 21 (May 1986) 213–232.
5. J. Conte and D. Sexton, "Relationship of Adult Sexual Abuse Survivors to Adult Children of Alcoholics" (Accepted for publication in *Journal for Interpersonal Violence,* 1991).
6. S. M. Sgroi, *Handbook of Clinical Intervention in Child Sexual Abuse* (Lexington, Mass.: Lexington Books, 1982).

3

Moving On
in Recovery

I wrote *Double Duty* out of my conviction that no one should have to go through life with the shame that is created in dysfunctional families. It is my belief that once we are able to understand the dynamics of our Adult Child issues, we can truly begin to work through them. In the life stories you have just read, you've seen how people have chosen various means of working through their issues. It is possible for each and every one of us to have recovery. We no longer have to live our lives based in fear.

The process of recovery allows us to put the negative influences of our past behind us and take responsibility for how we live our life today. It is a process that takes time, patience, and persistence. To put our past behind us, we must come out of denial and begin to speak the truth about our life experiences. We can no longer minimize, rationalize, or discount what really happened to us. We must own our experiences.

The Stages and Steps of Recovery

People tend to move through five distinct stages in the process of Adult Child recovery. The stages presented are a synthesis from the works of Julie Bowden and Herb Gravitz, authors of *Guide to Recovery*.

FIRST STAGE: SURVIVORSHIP

We begin by knowing that we can and will survive. While Adult Children deserve to feel good about their survivorship, they also deserve more in life.

SECOND STAGE: EMERGENT AWARENESS

This is where we recognize that there was something wrong in our childhood and we no longer deny it. We are free to acknowledge our experience and its effects on us. This is often an exhilarating stage—a time in which we feel a sense of direction and hope.

THIRD STAGE: ADDRESSING CORE ISSUES

Once Adult Children have accepted the influence of the past on their lives, they are ready to confront the core issues that have plagued them as adults. It is in this stage that the Adult Child is most apt to need the assistance of others to work through such issues as control; identifying and expressing feelings; needs; limit setting and establishing boundaries; and self-validation. Throughout the entire process the Adult Child is working on trust and shame.

FOURTH STAGE: TRANSFORMATION

This is a time of personal change, of putting into effect the things we've been learning, of risking new behaviors. Transformation leads to internal integration. The work on previous stages has helped us to trust our internal wisdom, and we are now in the process of discarding hurtful beliefs and replacing them with beliefs that nurture loving self-acceptance and self-care.

FIFTH STAGE: GENESIS

Although this is different for each person, Genesis generally involves a new openness to the spiritual aspects of life. This is when we begin to participate in the creation of our own world—not grandiosely, but realistically. Genesis marks the true beginning of our lives as expressed through our unique relationship to the rest of the universe.

As part of the process of working through these recovery stages, I have identified four steps that need to be repeated, often more than once, with each and every issue one is addressing. The four steps are:

- Explore the past
- Connect the past with the present
- Challenge the belief messages
- Learn new skills

EXPLORE THE PAST

Much of the initial process of recovery involves talking about the past. Many people find this both exciting and scary, but the purpose of talking about the past is to put it behind us. This is not meant to be a blaming process; it is the process of speaking your own emotional truth. You talk about the past to undo denial.

This is very important because it is often the first

time in our lives that we have been able to talk openly about our experiences. Talking without fear of being rejected or punished allows us to release deep feelings that we have kept inside and that remain hurtful to us. When we do this with others who are participating in the same process, we receive validation for ourselves when we were young.

Most Adult Children have a skewed sense of what "normal" is. Only by talking about our experiences can we put them in a context that helps us recognize our needs and learn how to set appropriate limits and boundaries. More important, we are able to discard the messages that we aren't good enough or that we are inadequate. We begin to feel that we are of real value.

The grieving process is the most emotionally painful part of recovery. It can take months. At times Adult Children have been criticized for focusing on the past too much or for "staying in the problem," as opposed to searching for a solution. However, at this point we are in the process of owning our childhood experiences, and this takes a great deal of time. We don't remember everything all at one time, nor do all of our feelings come to the surface at once.

Adult Children need to own their fears, sadness, hurt, and anger. You don't necessarily want to do that with your parents, but you will want to do it with a counselor, other recovering Adult Children, or a trusted friend. We need to feel safe to be able to trust and to share our vulnerabilities. That can take time.

When we are exploring the past we are doing our "grief work," we are speaking of the losses in our lives. Because the pain of these losses has not been acknowledged or validated, taking the time to grieve for ourselves is important. Left unexamined, these feelings of loss grow into emotional time bombs that can become extremely hurtful if they have no appropriate avenues for expression. We act them out in depression, addictions, compulsive behaviors, hurtful relationships, difficulties with parenting, and so on. It is important that one ultimately moves beyond this first step. If not, you will become stuck in the process and it will become a blaming process, not a grief process.

CONNECT THE PAST WITH THE PRESENT

Another important step in recovery is that of connecting our past with our present. Here, the process focuses on insights. This is where we need to ask ourselves, "How does the past connect with who I am today?" Then we follow this with more and more specific questions.

"How does the fact that I spent so much time in isolation and in a fantasy world as a child affect me today?"

"How does the fact that I was so fearful of making a mistake in my childhood affect me today in my work?"

"How does the fact that I lived with so much fear as a child affect me in personal relationships today?"

We need to ask how our many feelings and behaviors in childhood and adolescence affect who we are today in all the many aspects of our lives, our self-esteem, our work, and our relationships. This allows us to focus more on the present.

CHALLENGE THE BELIEF MESSAGES

Early in the process of exploring the past, we also begin

to challenge the childhood beliefs we internalized from our parents. These are beliefs that we heard verbally or experienced behaviorally. Often the messages we internalized were parental "shoulds." "You shouldn't trust others." "You shouldn't be angry." "You shouldn't cry." So we need to go back and identify those internalized messages or life scripts. We need to ask ourselves whether those messages are helpful or hurtful, positive or negative. We need to question whether or not we want to continue to take these internalized messages with us throughout our adulthood.

Helpful messages would be:

All people deserve respect.
People are trustworthy.
You are of value.
It's okay to say No.

Hurtful messages we often heard were:

You can't trust anybody.
No one's going to be there for you.
You can't do anything about it, so don't bother.
Your needs are not important.

It's okay to keep the helpful messages. By acknowledging the ones we're going to keep, we take present-day ownership of them. They no longer belong just to our parents, they are ours as well.

The hurtful messages need to be discarded. This is often done in a symbolic form. For each message tossed out, you will need to create a new helpful one in its place. This is active recovery—you are taking responsibility for how you live your life.

LEARN NEW SKILLS

As we're reading, listening, and sharing, we're also taking another step. We're learning new skills. Much of recovery involves learning the skills we didn't get the chance to acquire in childhood. These are often such basics as:

Identifying feelings
Expressing feelings
Asking for help
Recognizing options
Problem-solving
Negotiating
Setting limits
Saying No
Saying Yes
Drawing attention to yourself in a positive way
Playing
Relaxing
Listening
Making a decision

Once we learn to use these skills, we're ready to live our lives differently. Now we have choices that haven't been there up to now.

With the healing that results from these four steps, Adult Children will free themselves from viewing life through the lens of addiction. Recovery leads to establishing a balance in life. While life will always pose certain restrictions and problems, the Adult Child now has a range of skills and the awareness of self to cope with and respond to the imperfections that come with life. Recovering does not mean you will never feel pain again, it doesn't guarantee good decisions nor prevent relationship break-ups. It won't necessarily give you the material things you desire. It will offer you an emotional freedom from the past, so that the past no longer dictates your self-worth and esteem. It will give you options; it empowers; it brings you into the "here and now."

In order to take these four steps, we need a continuous flow of information and support. Until the last few years we haven't had the information necessary even to understand what has been going on in our lives.

Recovery Literature

By reading books that support recovery, by attending lectures and workshops, and by becoming part of self-help groups or being in therapy, we can develop the language we need to begin talking about our experiences. We are people who spent our childhood years in sick families where people did not speak the truth and did not acknowledge what was occurring around them. We have so rigidly adhered to the "Don't talk," "Don't feel," "Don't think," "Don't ask questions" rules that, as adults, we really don't have the words or the understanding we need to describe our own experiences of the past or the present. Many Adult Children cannot discern one feeling from another. In addition, we often lack the ability to distinguish the normal from the abnormal.

Reading is often a good place to begin. It is a wonderful adjunct to both therapy and self-help recovery. It will familiarize you with the language that has become common to the recovery movement. More importantly, it will offer you a better understanding of what has happened in your life. Reading will allow your frozen feelings to thaw, and you will begin to realize that you don't have to continue your life with fear, shame, or other hurtful behaviors. Reading will show you that there is a path, a direction, out of the maze. It will help you realize that you are not alone.

As you read, you will begin to see yourself, and you will be amazed. It's as if the author had been raised in your home or had been living side by side with you in your adult life. Nearly every other Adult Child has felt as you have felt: guilty, ashamed, frightened, alone, sad, so unique. Reading helps to lessen that.

But be open to going beyond self-learning and insight. Allowing yourself access to others in recovery is wonderfully validating. It is also freeing to share your issues in the safety of rooms where so many others will identify with you.

Self-Help Groups

In general, self-help groups have been extremely valuable to thousands of people with various maladies. Adult Children have found support, validation, and direction in recovery through Al-Anon, Adult Children of Alcoholics, and Co-Dependents Anonymous. Although most Adult Children who mention participating in self-help groups are usually referring to the Twelve Step process, as you read this book you will see that others found self-help groups in different ways.

In coming together with other Adult Children in self-help groups, you will learn more about what all Adult Children have in common. Participants talk about their struggles and successes while developing problem-solving skills. They also find comfort in the fact that they are not unique, not alone in their problems. Most often the participants come to regard the group as a healthy extended family.

Whatever path you choose, remember, it is important to give self-help groups a fair chance before you say, "That's not for me." Try out different meetings. In Twelve Step meetings the group will often recommend that the newcomer try at least six meetings before making a decision about further participation.

It is common for Adult Children to want to work out problems on their own, to keep their feelings stuffed and controlled. We learned to master that approach a long time ago. But now we need to recognize that our old ways aren't working for us any longer. We need to keep an open mind. The simple act of sharing with another person who has had similar feelings and has encountered similar situations brings us out of denial and isolation. This kind of sharing also offers us a greater awareness of ourselves and a feeling of greater connectedness with others. Often a group experience allows us to accomplish together what we cannot do alone. This is true of both self-help and therapy groups.

Therapy

There are many different types of therapy. Many Adult Children have already spent considerable time in therapy long before they discovered they were ACOAs. It is important to choose a path of recovery that feels safe to you. If you have found therapy to be valuable in the past, then it is likely to be even more helpful now that you are exploring this new information. It is possible that if you seek a therapist who gives credence to Adult Child issues, your experience will be much richer and more beneficial.

The types of therapy available differ, depending on whether the therapists work with people individually or in groups. Some therapies focus on the here and now, dealing with a specific problem; others are more process-oriented. Some are conducted for a specific period of time with all participants having the same goals; others are more long term, with or without a closing date. Here, the participants all have similar backgrounds and similar goals, yet work on issues specific to themselves.

Should you want to talk to someone about the fact that you are an Adult Child, and discuss specific issues, I recommend that you begin in one of two places. First, ask other Adult Children you know if they are in therapy and whom they see. Ask them what they are getting out of therapy. What do they like and what do they not like about this specific therapist and the process? Acquire the names of two or three therapists and make an appointment with each one for an exploratory session. This is your time to ask the therapist questions, to decide if this is the right person to guide and support you in your recovery process. Some people can make this evaluation in a short telephone conversation; others require a face-to-face interview. The important thing is to find a therapist who feels right for you and then to allow yourself to make a commitment to the therapeutic process.

The second way to get a therapist is by calling an information and referral service knowledgeable about chemical dependency resources. This is most often the local council on alcoholism and a chemical dependency treatment program.

Crucial to your recovery is that your counselor or therapist understand the process of chemical dependency and Adult Child issues. In the exploratory sessions you can ask if they have done any reading in these areas. Have they taken specific training in this field? If the therapist discounts or minimizes addiction or ACOA issues, consider moving on to someone willing to address such issues in your therapy. You do not need to be with a therapist who works only with Adult Children. However, you do need someone sensitive to what being an ACOA means, someone knowledgeable about the dynamics of being raised in a chemically dependent home and the effects these have on your adult life.

Pacing Yourself

Although the timing of the issues to be addressed in the process of recovery may be different for the Dual Identity Adult Child who has a primary addiction, the process is similar.

Because of the intensification of effects experienced by those who are DD/DI, it is important that you not judge the pace at which you respond to a recovery program or compare your recovery rate with other people's. Often, the beginning weeks and months of recovery are the most difficult for DD/DI Adult Children because of their greater fear of giving up control and of trusting, along with their experiencing greater denial and, certainly, greater shame. Although you will walk through the same process as others, you may need to take more time to do so. All recovery is taken in steps, not leaps and bounds. But sometimes the DD/DI person may need to take baby steps.

In addition, you will also need to address the dynamics of the added trauma in your life—physical abuse and/or sexual abuse; being an only child; or having two chemically dependent parents. And you will need to address any identity issues—being gay, lesbian, physically disabled, or a person of color. After recognizing the similarities among Adult Children and addressing the issues common to all, DD/DI ACOAs will need to retrace their steps: explore the past, connect with the present, and challenge the shoulds as they relate to their DD/DI. These first three stages tend to take a longer period of time, but once they've been explored, "learning new skills" comes as readily to the DD/DI as to any Adult Child.

While I've said it many times in *Double Duty,* I would like to offer this advice one more time. If you don't feel safe in a group process, you may find that individual therapy offers you an added safety net. For those who participate in Twelve Step programs, the concept of individual sponsorship is highly beneficial. While there are many rewards in the group experience, if you don't feel comfortable with it, simply allow your self-awareness to direct you to what is most appropriate for fulfilling your present needs. Your recovery deserves to be safe. Be patient with yourself.

Resistances

The two greatest resistances to recovery are first, wanting the process to be pain free, and second, wanting to do it all by ourselves.

Adult Children often want recovery, but they'd like it without the pain. That's understandable. It's not been safe previously to feel; we feel out of control and bad for being emotional. And should we begin to get in touch with our feelings, we often feel years and years of pain, which seems overwhelming. But we *must walk through the pain* in order to put it behind us. Today we have the inner strength and can do it! As vulnerable as we feel, nothing bad has to happen to us. And that is certainly true when we allow others to be a part of our process—which puts us in contact with the second resistance—wanting to do recovery in isolation.

When we are frightened, we can easily fall back into our old pattern of solitary self-reliance. Now is the time to remind ourselves of the price we pay for isolation. It is my belief that, even if we could do recovery by ourselves, we deserve so much more. For far too long we have lived in isolation—if not social, then certainly emotional isolation. We deserve to give ourselves the rich experience of allowing others to be a part of our process. There are thousands of Adult Children in recovery today who would be willing to offer you support through both self-help and therapy groups. There are increasing numbers of educators, counselors, and therapists who are skilled in walking Adult Children through recovery. Other people can help make recovery a much easier and, very often, a much safer process.

A Word of Caution

Adult Children have a tendency to want to make decisions when they are in the midst of their feelings: "I feel sad, therefore I must _____." "I am angry, therefore I will _____." While feelings are cues and signals about our needs, it is important to not make any major life changes in early recovery.

At that point it is easy to find fault with much of how we live our lives. We tell ourselves: "I never would have chosen this partner ten years ago if I hadn't been so sick, so I must get out of this relationship." "My job is as sick as the family I was raised in. I want to change careers." "I need to be that child I was never allowed to be, so I'm going to walk away from my marriage and children and recapture my childhood."

Although your relationship and your job may have problems, or you want to go back to your childhood, making abrupt decisions in early recovery rarely leads to the dream scenario you have hoped for. Early recovery may bring many feelings and insights, but you haven't yet integrated the new skills that will enable you to live your life differently. When we make a change just "to make changes," we often end up re-creating a situation identical with the one we are escaping. Even more important, there is a tendency in early recovery to project feelings from our childhood onto present-day situations.

With time, such projections lessen, and what seemed

so bad is not nearly the crisis it first appeared to be. As you develop new skills, you will have the opportunity to act differently in your current relationships, at work, and with friends. At this later stage the decisions you make will be based more on choice. You may still choose to make certain changes, but they will be based more on your present-day perspective, more on the strong foundation of your ongoing recovery.

Love and Loyalty

While we can get very excited about recovery, telling the truth about our past often makes us feel disloyal to our family. After all, we love our parents. This is when we need to remember that being in recovery doesn't mean we don't love our parents. Most of us do. Often we have loved them against all odds, and that is why our hurts are so deep.

In recovery we aren't betraying those parts of our parents that truly loved us. Healthy parents love their children and want them to live free, happy lives. They don't want us to carry pain, fear, anguish, or loneliness with us. They want us to feel good about who we are. At this point in recovery the most important disloyalty to guard against is disloyalty to ourselves for not allowing ourselves a new way of life.

If your parents have continued to deteriorate in their disease, your new behavior will alter the nature of your relationship. Even if your parents have experienced recovery, your relationship may still need to be redefined. That can hurt. But whether or not your parents are in recovery, *you* can have recovery. And you can maintain a relationship with them if you choose. This relationship will have limitations—but the old relationship had limitations, too.

You may be wondering how many of your feelings and perceptions, if any, you might be able to share with your parents. Personally, I would not recommend that you share much of your experience with your parents in the early months of recovery. After that, what you share, how much you share, with whom and when, are important questions that need a great deal of thought. Generally speaking, we don't want to keep recovery a secret. At the same time, if our parents have remained sick, they will most likely respond hurtfully to any information we give them.

If you are thinking of talking directly to your parents about your recovery, consider approaching each parent separately. Then ask yourself: "What do I want to tell him (her)?" "Why do I want to say this?" "Will it help me if I say it?" "Am I saying it to hurt them?" "What do I hope will happen?" "How realistic are my expectations?" It is important to think ahead about what it is you want to disclose. "Living our recovery" as we relate to our parents is an even greater goal than sharing all of our feelings and thoughts with them.

The Reward for Going Deeper

So many feelings will awaken as you read this book and reflect on your own experiences. Please let me remind you again that, when you have bottled up your feelings for so long, it is easy to feel that you are losing control when they begin to well up. In the beginning we can feel overwhelmed by our emotions. Sometimes we don't even know what they are or why we are having them.

Don't be critical of yourself at this time. The fact that you are feeling is significant. Adult Children frequently have many feelings at one time. Often you may not know the exact source of the feeling as you experience it. Sometimes we only know what we feel after the fact. But if you keep talking, in time the source will connect with the feeling. Practice identifying your feelings and gradually experiment with telling someone about them.

As you move through recovery, ask yourself periodically which feelings are the easiest for you to show people and which are more difficult. What fears have you about showing the more difficult feelings? If you are frightened of showing your anger or sadness, ask yourself what you fear will happen if you show that feeling. Tell someone about the fears. Are your fears based on your present experience, or are they from your childhood? So often we have fears left over from long-ago experiences, but until we question them we don't realize it. Now ask yourself what you need to do to be able to express those feelings. Then give it a try.

The recovery process is often described as peeling an onion—below one layer there is another and then another. Looking at DD/DI issues brings us one layer closer to the core. When you work intensely on a particular area, there may be a deep pain associated with certain feelings for a period of time. Then there will be periods where your recovery enjoys smooth sailing. But again, unexpectedly, you will find yourself confronting another serious and painful issue. Remember: you haven't done anything wrong, you just couldn't have reached this layer of recovery before you addressed the other layers. Sometimes the reward for going deeper is going deeper. With each layer of recovery you are a step closer to resolving old issues and letting go of the past.

Strategies to Help with the Pitfalls

We all have particular pitfalls in recovery, but they aren't necessarily unique to us. There are clues common to many of us that can be used as signals to warn ourselves that we are slipping back into old behaviors or attitudes. It will be helpful for you to identify yours and know what you need to do when you recognize them.

Take a minute right now to finish the following sentence in at least four different ways.

"I know I'm in trouble when I _____."
"I know I'm in trouble when I _____."
"I know I'm in trouble when I _____."
"I know I'm in trouble when I _____."

So often I've heard people say, "I know I am in trouble when . . .

I isolate myself."
I minimize my feelings."
I start critical self-talk again."
I get overinvolved in such areas as work or fixing others."
I feel inadequate or inferior."
I don't want to trust anybody."

We can begin to avoid these potholes if we know what to look for. But we also need to plan out what we're going to do if we find ourselves there. So take your specific pitfalls and develop a strategy plan for each one.

Isolate. Have a list of phone numbers of people to call. Tell them of my behavior. Identify my most recent feelings or talk about what was occurring at the time I began to separate from my feelings.

Minimizing Feelings. What am I really feeling? What message am I sending myself right now that is making me stuff this feeling? I'm going to challenge that message because I know it's an old message from the past. What is it I've been learning lately about healthy feelings?

Critical Self-Talk. Stop!! Quit projecting. Recognize that I'm into "all or nothing" thinking again. What is it I'm feeling right this minute? Keep telling myself, "It's okay to make a mistake."

Overinvolvement. What am I avoiding? What am I running away from? Whose approval am I seeking?

Feeling Inadequate. I'm going to make an effort to spend time with recovering friends. I'm going to pay attention to my daily victories. I'll praise myself for them. I'll give myself healthy rewards.

Not Trusting Anybody. I recognize that the issue is "all or nothing." Whom do I trust now? What is it I trust about that person? What little things do I trust with other people?

* * *

Now you will have a list of warning signs and a set of new behaviors that you can act on to counteract those old attitudes and messages. Planning ahead makes it easier for you to respond in a healthy manner when the time comes. And those times will come. We are human. Many of us are recovering from terrifying childhoods. All of us are recovering from close to twenty years, if not more, of hurtful messages and coping skills that no longer work for us.

Recovery is a step-by-step process. It is hard work. It is exciting work. It can be emotionally painful at times. It can be confusing at times. But, ultimately, recovery is validating and extremely rewarding.

The *Next* Step

As recovering Adult Children, one of the things we learn about ourselves is that we are people of courage and strength. When we were children we had the courage and strength to endure. However we responded to the pain in our lives, it was our way of surviving. We found our lifelines and used them well.

But today, in recovery, we find that we often need to give up those defenses. This can be very difficult—for they have been our major form of protection. Yet, one by one, we find we have the courage to do just that. It is not possible to read Double Duty/Dual Identity life stories and not see the magnitude of pain induced without also recognizing the inner strength that guides us to seek out and travel the path to recovery that helps us to overcome the pain.

Recovery comes for the Double Duty/Dual Identity person as we embrace all of our being.

Our body.

Our culture.

Our vulnerability.

Our strengths—which we developed in response to the multiple issues we had to deal with in our lives.

While the following manifesto has relevance for us all, I created it for, dedicate and offer it to those who have struggled so long and so bravely with Double Duties and Dual Identities.

Double Duty/Dual Identity Manifesto

- I take responsibililty for how I live my life. I no longer walk through life hiding behind masks for self-protection.
- I no longer live a life based on fear and shame.
- I reject messages of shame, whether they come from others or through my own critical self-talk. I create affirming messages of love and empowerment.
- I am willing to ask for help. I am willing and able to include others in my process.
- I no longer accept a life of loneliness. Now I feel secure when I am alone, and comfort when I am with others.
- I am of value, and this remains true no matter what mistakes I might make.
- I trust in myself, and I trust in others.
- I no longer live in fear of being abandoned. I trust in my own value even when I feel the most vulnerable.

- I identify and establish healthy boundaries so I will not be violated, emotionally or physically. I am learning the skills I need to set the limits that maintain those boundaries.
- I identify and seek recovery from my compulsions, addictions, and self-defeating behaviors.
- I recognize I have choices and am willing to act on those choices. At the same time, I also recognize where my power lies.
- I take pride in my heritage. I acknowledge and embrace the healthy aspects of my culture.
- I no longer deny and reject parts of my physical being. I accept my body and find the strengths in my disabilities.
- I deserve to live a life unencumbered by sexual stigmas.
- I recognize and honor what is unique about myself and my personal history. I affirm the positives in my differences.
- I speak my truth.
- I recognize and celebrate my strengths.
- I believe in my right to happiness, dignity, and respect.
- I love and accept all of my self.

Appendixes

Anonymous Fellowship Acronyms

Common Acronyms of Twelve-Step Anonymous Fellowships Referred to within *Double Duty*:

AA	Alcoholics Anonymous
ACA	Adult Children of Alcoholics
ACOA	Adult Children of Alcoholics
CODA	Co-Dependents Anonymous
CA	Cocaine Anonymous
GA	Gamblers Anonymous
NA	Narcotics Anonymous
OA	Overeaters Anonymous

Appendix 1
The Twelve Steps of Alcoholics Anonymous

1. We admitted we were powerless over alcohol—that our lives had become unmanageable.
2. Came to believe that a Power greater than ourselves could restore us to sanity.
3. Made a decision to turn our will and our lives over to the care of God *as we understood Him.*
4. Made a searching and fearless moral inventory of ourselves.
5. Admitted to God, to ourselves, and to another human being the exact nature of our wrongs.
6. Were entirely ready to have God remove all these defects of character.
7. Humbly asked Him to remove our shortcomings.
8. Made a list of all persons we had harmed, and became willing to make amends to them all.
9. Made direct amends to such people wherever possible, except when to do so would injure them or others.
10. Continued to take personal inventory and when we were wrong promptly admitted it.
11. Sought through prayer and meditation to improve our conscious contact with God *as we understood Him,* praying only for knowledge of His will for us and the power to carry that out.
12. Having had a spiritual awakening as the result of these Steps, we tried to carry this message to alcoholics, and to practice these principles in all our affairs.

The Twelve Steps reprinted with permission of Alcoholics Anonymous World Services, Inc.

Appendix 2
The Twelve Traditions of Alcoholics Anonymous

1. Our common welfare should come first; personal recovery depends upon AA unity.
2. For our group purpose there is but one ultimate authority—a loving God as He may express Himself in our group conscience. Our leaders are but trusted servants; they do not govern.
3. The only requirement for AA membership is a desire to stop drinking.
4. Each group should be autonomous except in matters affecting other groups or AA as a whole.
5. Each group has but one primary purpose—to carry its message to the alcoholic who still suffers.
6. An AA group ought never endorse, finance, or lend the AA name to any related facility or outside enterprise, lest problems of money, property, and prestige divert us from our primary purpose.
7. Every AA group ought to be fully self-supporting, declining outside contributions.
8. Alcoholics Anonymous should remain forever nonprofessional, but our service centers may employ special workers.
9. AA, as such, ought never be organized; but we may create service boards or committees directly responsible to those they serve.

10. Alcoholics Anonymous has no opinion on outside issues; hence the AA name ought never be drawn into public controversy.
11. Our public relations policy is based on attraction rather than promotion; we need always maintain personal anonymity at the level of press, radio and films.
12. Anonymity is the spiritual foundation of all our Traditions, ever reminding us to place principles before personalities.

The Twelve Traditions reprinted with permission of Alcoholics Anonymous World Services, Inc.

Appendix 3
Do You Have the Disease of Alcoholism?

Alcoholism strikes one out of every ten people who drink. Not everyone has the physiological makeup to become alcoholic, but anyone who drinks could be at risk. Alcoholism doesn't discriminate. It afflicts people of all ethnic backgrounds, professions, and economic levels. It is not known precisely what causes this disease, but drinking is clearly a prerequisite. Therefore everyone who drinks should periodically evaluate their drinking patterns and behavior. Here is a self-test to help you review the role alcohol plays in your life. These questions incorporate many of the common symptoms of alcoholism. This test is intended to help you determine if you or someone you know needs to find out more about alcoholism; it is not intended to be used to establish the diagnosis of alcoholism.

YES NO

1. Do you ever drink heavily when you are disappointed, under pressure or have had a quarrel with someone?

164

                                                    YES NO

2. Can you handle more alcohol now than when   __ __
   you first started to drink?

3. Have you ever been unable to remember part   __ __
   of the previous evening, even though your
   friends say you didn't pass out?

4. When drinking with other people, do you try __ __
   to have a few extra drinks when others won't
   know about it?

5. Do you sometimes feel uncomfortable if al-   __ __
   cohol is not available?

6. Are you in more of a hurry to get your first __ __
   drink of the day than you used to be?

7. Do you sometimes feel a little guilty about __ __
   your drinking?

8. Has a family member or close friend ever ex- __ __
   pressed concern or complained about your
   drinking?

9. Have you been having more memory "black-   __ __
   outs" recently?

10. Do you often want to continue drinking after __ __
    your friends say they have had enough?

11. Do you usually have a reason for the occasions __ __
    when you drink heavily?

12. When you are sober, do you often regret things __ __
    you have done or said while you were drinking?

13. Have you ever switched brands or drinks following __ __
    different plans to control your drinking?

14. Have you sometimes failed to keep the prom- __ __
    ises you have made to yourself about control-
    ling or cutting down on your drinking?

15. Have you ever had a DWI (driving while   __ __
    intoxicated) or DUI (driving under the influence
    of alcohol) violation, or any other legal prob-
    lem related to your drinking?

16. Do you try to avoid family or close friends __ __
    while you are drinking?

17. Are you having more financial, work, school __ __
    and/or family problems as a result of your
    drinking?

YES NO

18. Has your physician ever advised you to cut ___ ___
    down on your drinking?
19. Do you eat very little or irregularly during the ___ ___
    periods when you are drinking?
20. Do you sometimes have the "shakes" in the ___ ___
    morning and find that it helps to have a "lit-
    tle" drink, tranquilizer or medication of some
    kind?
21. Have you recently noticed that you cannot ___ ___
    drink as much as you once did?
22. Do you sometimes stay drunk for several days ___ ___
    at a time?
23. After periods of drinking do you sometimes ___ ___
    see or hear things that aren't there?
24. Have you ever gone to anyone for help about ___ ___
    your drinking?
25. Do you ever feel depressed or anxious before, ___ ___
    during or after periods of heavy drinking?
26. Have any of your blood relatives ever had a ___ ___
    problem with alcohol?

Any "Yes" answer indicates a probable symptom of alcoholism. "Yes" answers to several of the questions indicate the following stages of alcoholism:

Questions 1 to 8: Early stage.
Questions 9 to 21: Middle stage.
Questions 22 to 26: Beginning of final stage.

Appendix 4
Relationship Addiction

	YES	NO
1. Typically, you come from a dysfunctional home in which your emotional needs were not met.	___	___
2. Having received little real nurturing yourself, you try to fill this unmet need vicariously by becoming a care-giver, especially to men who appear, in some way, needy.	___	___
3. Because you were never able to change your parent(s) into the warm, loving caretaker(s) you longed for, you respond deeply to the familiar type of emotionally unavailable man whom you can again try to change, through your love.	___	___
4. Terrified of abandonment, you will do anything to keep a relationship from dissolving.	___	___
5. Almost nothing is too much trouble, takes too much time, or is too expensive if it will "help" the man you are involved with.	___	___
6. Accustomed to lack of love in personal relationships, you are willing to wait, hope, and try harder to please.		

YES NO

7. You are willing to take far more than 50 percent of the responsibility, guilt, and blame in any relationship. ___ ___

8. Your self-esteem is critically low, and deep inside you do not believe you deserve to be happy. Rather, you believe you must earn the right to enjoy life. ___ ___

9. You have a desperate need to control your men and your relationships, having experienced little security in childhood. You mask your efforts to control people and situations as "being helpful." ___ ___

10. In a relationship, you are much more in touch with your dream of how it could be than with the reality of your situation. ___ ___

11. You are addicted to men and to emotional pain. ___ ___

12. You may be predisposed emotionally and often biochemically to becoming addicted to drugs, alcohol, and/or certain foods, particularly sugary ones. ___ ___

13. By being drawn to people with problems that need fixing, or by being enmeshed in situations that are chaotic, uncertain, and emotionally painful, you avoid focusing on your responsibility to yourself. ___ ___

14. You may have a tendency toward episodes of depression, which you try to forestall through the excitement provided by an unstable relationship. ___ ___

15. You are not attracted to men who are kind, stable, reliable, and interested in you. You find such "nice" men boring. ___ ___

Source: Robin Norwood, Women Who Love Too Much *(Los Angeles: Tarcher, 1985), 10–11. Reprinted with permission.*

Appendix 5
Are You a Food Addict?

		YES	NO
1.	Are you intensely afraid of becoming fat?	__	__
2.	Do you feel fat even when others say you are thin or emaciated?	__	__
3.	Do you like to shop for food and cook for others but prefer not to eat the meals you make?	__	__
4.	Do you have eating rituals (for example, cutting food into tiny bites, eating only certain foods in a certain order at a particular time of day)?	__	__
5.	Have you lost 25 percent of your minimum body weight through diets and fasts?	__	__
6.	When you feel hungry, do you usually refrain from eating?	__	__
7.	If you are a female of childbearing age, have you stopped having menstrual periods?	__	__
8.	Do you often experience cold hands and feet, dry skin, or cracked fingernails?	__	__
9.	Do you have a covering of fuzzy hair over your body?	__	__
10.	Do you often feel depressed, guilty, angry, or inadequate?	__	__

YES   NO

11. When people express concern about your low weight, do you deny that anything is wrong? ___ ___

12. Do you often exercise strenuously or for long periods of time even when you feel tired or sick? ___ ___

13. Have you ever eaten a large amount of food and then fasted, forced yourself to vomit, or used laxatives to purge yourself? ___ ___

14. Are you frequently on a rigid diet? ___ ___

15. Do you regularly experience stomachaches or constipation? ___ ___

16. Do you eat large quantities of food in a short period of time, usually high-calorie, simple-carbohydrate foods that can be easily ingested (for example, bread, pasta, cake, cookies, ice cream, or mashed potatoes)? ___ ___

17. Do you eat in secret, hide food, or lie about your eating? ___ ___

18. Have you ever stolen food or money to buy food so that you could start or continue a binge? ___ ___

19. Do you feel guilt and remorse about your eating behavior? ___ ___

20. Do you start eating even when you are not hungry? ___ ___

21. Is it hard for you to stop eating even when you want to? ___ ___

22. Do you eat to escape problems, to relax, or to have fun? ___ ___

23. After finishing a meal, do you worry about making it to the next meal without getting hungry in between? ___ ___

24. Have others expressed concern about your obsession with food? ___ ___

25. Do you worry that your eating behavior is abnormal? ___ ___

26. Do you fall asleep after eating? ___ ___

27. Do you regularly fast, use laxatives or diet pills, induce vomiting, or exercise excessively to avoid gaining weight?

YES NO

28. Does your weight fluctuate ten pounds or more   __ __
    from alternate bingeing and purging?   __ __
29. Are your neck glands swollen?
30. Do you have scars on the back of your hands   __ __
    from forced vomiting?

SCORING: *Five or more "Yes" answers within any of the following three groups of questions strongly suggest the presence of an eating disorder: questions 1–15, anorexia nervosa; questions 14–26, binge eating; questions 12–30, bulimia.*

Appendix 6
The Original Laundry List—
Adult Children of Alcoholics

THE PROBLEM
The characteristics we seem to have in common due to our being brought up in an alcoholic household:

A. We became isolated and afraid of people and authority figures.
B. We became approval seekers and lost our identity in the process.
C. We are frightened by angry people and any personal criticism.
D. We either become alcoholics, marry them, or both, or find another compulsive personality such as a workaholic to fulfill our sick abandonment needs.
E. We live life from the viewpoint of victims and are attracted by that weakness in our love and friendship relationships.
F. We have an overdeveloped sense of responsibility and it is easier for us to be concerned with others rather than ourselves; this enables us not to look too closely at our own faults, etc.

G. We get guilt feelings when we stand up for ourselves instead of giving in to others.

H. We became addicted to excitement.

I. We confuse love and pity and tend to "love" people we can "pity" and "rescue."

J. We have stuffed our feelings from our traumatic childhoods and have lost the ability to feel or express our feelings because it hurts so much. (Denial)

K. We judge ourselves harshly and have a very low sense of self-esteem.

L. We are dependent personalities who are terrified of abandonment and will do anything to hold on to a relationship in order not to experience painful abandonment feelings that we received from living with sick people who were never there emotionally for us.

M. Alcoholism is a family disease and we became para-alcoholics and took on the characteristics of that disease even though we did not pick up the drink.

N. Para-alcoholics are reactors rather than actors.

THE SOLUTION

By attending Adult Children of Alcoholics meetings on a regular basis, we learn that we can live our lives in a more meaningful manner; we learn to change our attitudes and old patterns of behavior and habits; to find serenity, even happiness.

A. Alcoholism is a *three-fold disease*: mental, physical, and spiritual; our parents were victims of this disease, which either ends in death or insanity. This is the beginning of the gift of forgiveness.

B. We learn to put the focus on ourselves and to be good to ourselves.

C. We learn to detach with love; tough love.

D. We use the slogans: LET GO, LET GOD; EASY DOES IT; ONE DAY AT A TIME, etc.

E. We learn to feel our feelings, to accept and express them, and to build our self-esteem.

F. Through working the steps, we learn to accept the disease and to realize that our lives have become unmanageable and that we are powerless over the disease and the alcoholic. As we become willing to admit our defects and our sick thinking, we are able to change our attitudes and our reactions into actions. By working the program daily, admitting that we are powerless; we come to believe eventually in the spirituality of the program—that there is a solution other than ourselves, the group, a Higher Power, God as we understand Him, Her or It. By sharing our experiences, relating to others, welcoming newcomers, serving our groups, we build our self-esteem.

G. We learn to love ourselves and in this way we are able to love others in a healthier way.

H. We use telephone therapy with program people who understand us.

I.   The serenity prayer is our major prayer.

Appendix 7
Professional Resources

Anorexia Nervosa and
   Related Eating Disorders
   (ANRED)
P.O. Box 5102
Eugene, Oregon 97405
(503)344-1144

Cocaine Hotline
   (800)662-HELP

Children of Alcoholics
   Foundation (CAF)
200 Park Avenue, 31st Floor
New York, NY 10166
(212)351-2680

Institute on Black Chemical
   Abuse (IBCA)
2614 Nicollet Avenue South
Minneapolis, MN 55408
(612)871-7878

National Asian Pacific
   Families Against
   Substance Abuse
   (NAPAFASA)
6303 Friendship Court
Bethesda, MD 20817
(301)530-0945

National Association of
   Anorexia Nervosa and
   Associated Disorders
   (ANAD)
P.O. Box 7
Highland Park, IL 60611
(708)831-3438

National Association of
   Children of Alcoholics
   (NACOA)
31582 Coast Highway
Suite B
South Laguna Beach,
   CA 92677
(714)499-3889

National Association of
  Lesbian and Gay
  Alcoholism Professionals
  (NALGAP)
204 West 20th Street
New York, NY 10011
(212)713-5074

National Black Alcoholism
  Council (NBAC)
417 South Dearborn Street,
  Suite 1000
Chicago, IL 60605
(312)663-5780

National Coalition Against
  Domestic Violence
1500 Massachusetts Avenue
  NW, Suite 35
Washington, DC 20005
(202)638-6388

National Coalition of
  Hispanic Health and
  Human Services
  Organization
(COSSMHO)
1030 15th Street NW,
  St. 1053
Washington, DC 20005
(202)371-2100

National Hispanic Family
  Against Drug Abuse
  (NHFADA)
1511 K Street, Suite 1029
Washington, DC 20005
(202)393-5136

Native American
  Association for Children
  of Alcoholics
  (NANACOA)
P.O. Box 18736
Seattle, WA 98118

Parents United
AMACU Coordinator
P.O. Box 952
San Jose, CA 95108
(408)453-7611, ext. 150
Treatment oriented

Phobia Society of America
133 Rollins Avenue,
  Suite 4B
Rockville, MD 20852
(301)231-9350

Victims of Incest Can
  Emerge Survivors in
  Action (VOICES)
Voices in Action, Inc.
P.O. Box 148309
Chicago, IL 60614
(312)327-1500

Appendix 8
Self-Help Groups Based on the
Twelve Step Program of AA

ACOA Intergroup of Greater
   New York, Inc.
P.O. Box 363
Murray Hill Station
New York, NY 10016-0363
(212)582-0840

Adult Children of
   Alcoholics (ACA)
2225 Sepulveda Blvd., #200
Torrance, CA 90505
(213)534-1815

Al-Anon Family Groups
P.O. Box 862
Midtown Station
New York, NY 10018-0862
(212)302-7240

Alateen
Al-Anon Family Groups
P.O. Box 862
Midtown Station
New York, NY 10018-0862
(212)302-7240

Alcoholics Anonymous (AA)
Box 459
Grand Central Station
New York, NY 10163
(212)686-1100

Anorexics/Bulimics
   Anonymous (ABA)
P.O. Box 112214
San Diego, CA 92111
(619)273-3108

DOUBLE DUTY: SEXUALLY ABUSED

Batterers Anonymous (BA)
BA Press
1269 NE Street
San Bernandino, CA 92405
(714)884-6809

Cocaine Anonymous (CA)
6125 Washington Blvd.,
    Suite 202
Los Angeles, CA 90230
(213)559-5833

Co-Dependents Anonymous
    (CODA)
P.O. Box 5508
Glendale, AZ 85312-5508
(602)979-1751

Gamblers Anonymous (GA)
National Service Office
P.O. Box 17173
Los Angeles, CA 90017
(213)386-8789

Narcotics Anonymous (NA)
World Services Office
16155 Wyandotte Street
Van Nuys, CA 91406
(818)780-3951

Overeaters Anonymous (OA)
World Services Office
4025 Spencer Street,
    Suite 203
Torrance, CA 90503
(213)542-8363

Parents Anonymous (PA)
6733 South Sepulveda Blvd.
Los Angeles, CA 90045
(213)410-9732
(800)421-0353

Sex Addicts Anonymous
    (SAA)
Box 3038
Minneapolis, MN 55403
(612)339-0217

Sexaholics Anonymous (SA)
P.O. Box 300
Simi Valley, CA 93062
(805)584-3235

Sex and Love Addicts
    Anonymous (SLAA)
(The Augustine Fellowship)
P.O. Box 119
New Town Branch
Boston, MA 02258
(617)332-1845

Survivors of Incest
    Anonymous (SIA)
P.O. Box 21817
Baltimore, MD 21222
(301)282-3400

Women for Sobriety
Box 618
Quakertown, PA 18951
(215)536-8026

Bibliography

EATING DISORDERS

Hampshire, Elizabeth. *Freedom from Food*. Park Ridge, Ill.: Parkside Publishers, 1987.

Hollis, Judi. *Fat Is a Family Affair*. New York: Harper & Row, 1988.

Orbach, Susie. *Fat Is a Feminist Issue: The Anti-Diet Guide to Permanent Weight Loss*. New York: Berkley Publishing Group, 1987.

Roth, Geneen. *Breaking Free From Compulsive Eating*. New York: New American Library, 1985.

———. *Feeding the Hungry Heart*. New York: New American Library, 1982.

———. *Why Weight? A Guide to Ending Compulsive Eating*. New York: New American Library, 1989.

SEXUAL ABUSE

Bass, Ellen, and Laura Davis. *The Courage to Heal: A Guide for Women Survivors of Child Sexual Abuse*. New York: Harper & Row, 1988.

Blume, E. Sue. *Secret Survivors: Uncovering Incest and Its Aftereffects in Women*. New York: John Wiley & Sons, 1990.

Crewdson, John. *By Silence Betrayed*. Boston: Little Brown, 1988.

Davis, Laura. *Allies in Healing: When the Person You Love was Sexually Abused as a Child, A Support Book for Partners*. New York: *Harper Collins*, 1991.

180 DOUBLE DUTY: SEXUALLY ABUSED

180 DOUBLE DUTY: SEXUALLY ABUSED

180 DOUBLE DUTY: SEXUALLY ABUSED

——. *The Courage to Heal Workbook.* New York: Harper & Row, 1988.

Engel, Beverly. *The Right to Innocence.* New York: Fawcett, 1989.

Gil, Eliana. *Outgrowing the Pain.* New York: Dell, 1988.

Lew, Michael. *Victims No Longer.* New York: Harper & Row, 1990.

Maltz, Wendy and Beverly Holman. *Incest and Sexuality: A Guide to Understanding and Healing.* New York: Free Press, 1986.

ADULT CHILDREN AND CO-DEPENDENTS

Ackerman, Robert. *Growing in the Shadow.* Deerfield Beach, Fla.: Health Communications, Inc., 1986.

——. *Let Go & Grow: Recovery for Adult Children.* Deerfield Beach, Fla.: Health Communications, Inc., 1987.

——. *Same House, Different Home.* Deerfield Beach, Fla.: Health Communications, Inc., 1987.

Beattie, Melody. *Beyond Codependency: And Getting Better All the Time.* Center City, Minn.: Hazelden Publishing, 1989.

——. *Codependent No More: How to Stop Controlling and Start Caring for Yourself.* New York: Harper & Row, 1988.

Black, Claudia. *"It Will Never Happen to Me."* New York: Ballantine Books, 1987.

——. *"My Dad Loves Me, My Dad Has a Disease."* Denver, Colo.: MAC Pub., 1979.

——. *Repeat After Me.* Denver, Colo.: MAC Pub., 1985.

Bradshaw, John. *Bradshaw on the Family: A Revolutionary Way of Self-Discovery.* Deerfield Beach, Fla.: Health Communications, Inc., 1988.

——. *Homecoming: Reclaiming and Championing Your Inner Child.* New York: Bantam, 1990.

Cermak, Timmen L. *Time to Heal: The Road to Recovery for Adult Children of Alcoholics.* Los Angeles: Jeremy P. Tarcher, Inc., 1988.

Fossum, Merle A., and Marilyn J. Mason. *Facing Shame: Families in Recovery.* New York: W. W. Norton & Co., 1986.

Gravitz, Herbert L., and Julie D. Bowden. *Guide to Recovery: A Book for Adult Children of Alcoholics.* Holmes Beach, Fla.: Learning Publications, Inc., 1986.

Greenleaf, Jael. *Co-Alcoholic, Para-Alcoholic: Who's Who and What's the Difference.* Denver, Colo.: MAC Pub., 1987.

Halvorson, Ronald S., and Valerie B. Deilgat, eds., with "Friends in Recovery" staff. *Twelve Steps—A Way Out: A Working Guide for Adult Children of Alcoholics and Other Dysfunctional Families.* San Diego, Calif.: Recovery Publications, 1987.

Kritsberg, Wayne. *The ACOA Syndrome.* Deerfield Beach, Fla.: Health Communications, Inc., 1985.

Middelton-Moz, Jane, and Lorie Dwinell. *After the Tears.* Deerfield Beach, Fla.: Health Communications, Inc., 1986.

Norwood, Robin. *Women Who Love Too Much.* New York: Pocket Books, 1986.

O'Gorman, Patricia, and Phil Oliver Diaz. *Self-Parenting.* Deerfield Beach, Fla.: Health Communications, Inc., 1988.

Robinson, Bryan E. *Working with Children of Alcoholics.* Lexington, Mass.: Lexington Books, 1989.

Sanford, Linda. *Strong at the Broken Places.* New York: Random House, 1990.

Smith, Ann. *Grandchildren of Alcoholics.* Deerfield Beach, Fla.: Health Communications, Inc., 1988.

Striano, Judi. *How to Find a Good Psychotherapist: A Consumer Guide.* Santa Barbara, Calif.: Professional Press, 1987.

Subby, Robert. *Lost in the Shuffle.* Deerfield Beach, Fla.: Health Communications, Inc., 1987.

Wegscheider-Cruse, Sharon. *Choicemaking.* Deerfield Beach, Fla.: Health Communications, Inc., 1985.

Whitfield, Charles L. *Healing the Child Within.* Deerfield Beach, Fla.: Health Communications, Inc., 1987.

——. *Co-Dependency: Healing the Human Condition.* Deerfield Beach, Fla.: Health Communications, Inc., 1991.

Woititz, Janet G. *Adult Children of Alcoholics.* Deerfield Beach, Fla.: Health Communications, Inc., 1983.

——. *Healing Your Sexual Self.* Deerfield Beach, Fla.: Health Communications, Inc., 1989.

——. *Struggle for Intimacy.* Deerfield Beach, Fla.: Health Communications, Inc., 1985.

RELATIONSHIPS

Covington, Stephanie, and Liana Beckett. *Leaving the Enchanted Forest.* New York: Harper & Row, 1988.

Cruse, Joe. *Painful Affairs.* Deerfield Beach, Fla.: Health Communications, Inc., 1988.

Lerner, Harriet G. *Dance of Anger: A Woman's Guide to Chang-*

ing the Patterns of Intimate Relationships. New York: Harper & Row, 1986.

Wegscheider-Cruse, Sharon. *Coupleship: How to Have a Relationship.* Deerfield Beach, Fla.: Health Communications, Inc., 1988.

INSPIRATIONAL

Black, Claudia. *"It's Never Too Late to Have a Happy Childhood."* New York: Ballantine Books, 1989.

Lerner, Rokelle. *Daily Affirmations.* Deerfield Beach, Fla.: Health Communications, Inc., 1985.

Somers, Suzanne. *Keeping Secrets.* New York: Warner Books, 1988.

Wegscheider-Cruse, Sharon. *Miracle of Recovery.* Deerfield Beach, Fla.: Health Communications, Inc., 1989.

Index

SOBERING INSIGHT FOR THE ALCOHOLIC . . . AND THE LOVED ONES WHO WANT TO HELP THEM